Handing Down

A Legacy of Blessings:

Things I Want You To

KNOW

What I Hope You Will

BE

&

Things I Hope You Will

DO

Paperback ISBN: 978-1-7338666-2-0

Publisher: Gloria J Rayborn

Scripture quotations are primarily from the King James Version of the Bible.

Scripture taken from *The Message*. Copyright © 1993, 1994, 1995, 1996, 2000, 2001, 2002. Used by permission of NavPress Publishing Group.

Scripture taken from the Amplified Bible, Copyright © 1954, 1958, 1952, 1964, 1965, 1987 by The Lockman Foundation. Used by permission.

This book is dedicated to my children who have inspired and encouraged me throughout their lifetime, and to my grandchildren who continue to bring so much joy to my life. I continue to learn something new from you every day. I love you all and thank God for blessing me with you.

This book would not be possible without God's loving kindness, saving grace through Jesus Christ, His faithfulness, truth, and leading of the Holy Spirit. May God be glorified in this book and use it to draw the readers closer to Him.

Other books written by Gloria Rayborn include:

"I Am Special"

"Sharing"

"Let's Go On a Treasure Hunt: Searching for Hidden Treasure"

TABLE OF CONTENTS

Introduction

Life is a journey. We each have a limited amount of time to live and fulfill our purpose. My journey has been filled with many ups and downs and has been an interesting one. I'm happy to say there have been more "ups" than "downs." I'm still learning and growing. Through years of observations, various teachings, and in reading the Bible, it has become clear to me how important it is to share what I've learned with you.

One of my key "takeaways" is how important "blessings" are to individuals and to families. Blessings in the Bible were always spoken or pronounced. They were spoken by the head of the family to children as well as to their children's descendants. Blessing children included willing them property as well as imparting words of wisdom, encouragement, and instructions -- which often painted a verbal picture of their future as well as their potential. The verbal picture of their future was based on God's plans for their lives. The names given to their children also had meanings that portrayed their blessing.

I believe it is possible for each of us to create a legacy for the next generation. A legacy is similar to a blessing. It is something –

money, property, wisdom, reputation, etc. -- that is handed down from one person or generation to another. The legacy can be good or bad, depending on the person.

I am leaving you a legacy and a blessing by sharing some of the things I've learned. The Bible teaches that a good person leaves an inheritance for their children's children (Proverbs 13:22). I've grouped these learnings into three main concepts: things I want you to **KNOW**, what I hope you will **BE**, and things I hope you will **DO** in life.

This book is **not** designed to cover everything you will experience in life. Please do not let this book become a substitute for studying the Bible nor from learning from others. I am just highlighting some of the things that I believe will help you. I do not have formal biblical training. I've been saved for 40+ years and have studied the Bible, but I still have more to learn. I've used scripture references for a number of these learnings. The scriptures I used are not exhaustive, so feel free to supplement this with additional scriptures as you go through this journey. You will find a concordance can be helpful in finding scriptures on various topics. It is also vital that you learn from others who have more in-depth knowledge of the Word of God.

Beware, there will be some things in this book that may not make sense to you right now. When I was young, my parents told me things that I thought were not right or were confusing. There were even times when I felt they didn't know what they were talking about; but now, I understand what they meant. Some of the things I'm sharing will only make sense as you encounter different life experiences. My hope is that at the right time, most, if not all of this information will enlighten you, too.

I suggest you first read through the book from cover to cover, and as you read **highlight** the points you have questions about or want to study more and write them down at the end of each section. Your first reading can be with or without looking up the scripture references. Once you've done your first reading, then focus on the areas you have highlighted and study the verse(s) included in that section. Seek assistance from your parents, do more research on the topic, and talk to your pastor or people who have a close relationship with God. I encourage your parents to use this as a guide to help you along your life's journey. Feel free to reach out to me and we can walk through this together.

I've learned that sometimes we get so caught up in worrying about what other people think about us and what they say that it eventually affects our self-esteem. At the end of Chapter 6, I've included something that I hope you will study and incorporate into your life. Let these words become a part of who you are. I call them "God's Designer Labels." I want you to wear these labels rather than any negative labels people will try to assign to you. It's up to you to determine which ones in life you will wear. Choose wisely!

As a bonus, I've also added some tips called "GGs Life Nuggets," which I believe will enhance your journey. As you learn and gain additional insights, please capture your learnings in writing and pass them on to the next generation(s).

Finally, I'm sharing **a written blessing** that I developed years ago for my family. You may wish to use it as inspiration to develop a blessing for your family. Most importantly, I hope you will receive and walk in this blessing.

PART I: Things I Want You to KNOW

Chapter 1: Know Who God Is

We will never fully understand God. He has revealed Himself as:

- **Our creator** -"In the beginning God created the heaven and the earth." (Genesis 1:1-31; John 1:1-5; Colossians1:16-17). As the creator, God designed His creation to work a certain way. He knows what is best for it and what causes it to flourish. Since God created the world and everything in it, He is the only one who knows how to optimize His creation and make it excel. Today, when people create products, they include a user's manual, and tell you how to assemble an item, point out what to do when things go wrong and give you operating procedures. God, as our creator, has given us His instruction manual in the Holy Bible. He has outlined what caused the problem – sin -- and provided the only solution – Jesus Christ.

- **Our Father -** (Matthew 5:45; 6:1-9; 7:11; 11:25-27; 12:50; 13:43...) and our **Adopter -** (Romans 8:15-23; Galatians 4:1-7; Ephesians 1:3-5). God is a good father. He draws us to Jesus (John 6:44; 6:65)

- **Everlasting –** The Bible doesn't say where God came from. It tells us that He was in the beginning. The Bible does say that God is everlasting (Genesis 21:33; Deuteronomy 33:27; Psalm 90:2; 93:2; 106:48). His mercy is everlasting and his truth endures to all generations (Psalm 100:5; 103:17-18).

- **Love -** (John 3:16; 1 John 4:8 and 1 John 4:16). Jesus came because of God's love.

- **Good and the giver of every perfect gift -** (Deuteronomy 26:11; Psalm 33:5; Matthew 7:11; John 3:16; James 1:17)

- **All knowing, all powerful, all seeing, and all present -** (Proverbs 15:3). God looks at the heart and not the outward appearance. (1 Samuel 16:7). Nothing is hidden from God. (Job 24:1; Isaiah 48:1-6)

- **Faithful -** (1 Corinthians 1:9; and 1 Corinthians 10:13; Hebrews 10:23; 1 John 1:9). God is faithful even when we are not. He is faithful to fulfill his promise, even though it may take longer than we think it should take. (1 Kings 8:56; 2 Chronicles 1:9; Psalm 105; Acts 1 & 2; 7:15-17; 13:17-24; Galatians 3:18-22; Hebrews 6:13-20; 10: 36-39; 2 Peter 1:3-4; 3:4-15; 1 John 2:25)

- **I AM** – the God of Abraham (Genesis 26:24); the God of Abraham and Isaac (Genesis 28:13). I am God, the God of thy father (Genesis 46:3) "I am the God of thy father, the God of Abraham, the God of Isaac, and the God of Jacob (Exodus 3:6). "And God said unto Moses, I AM THAT I AM; and he said, Thus shalt thou say unto the children of Israel, I AM hath sent me unto you" (Exodus 3:14). I AM is present tense. God does not change (Malachi 3:6). Jesus is the same yesterday, today and forever. (Hebrews 13:8). God is all we need.

- **Almighty -** (Genesis 17:1; 35:11). Nothing is impossible with God. (Matthew 19:26; Mark 9:23; 10:27; 14:36; Luke 1:37)

- **Most high** – (Genesis 14:18-22; Numbers 24:16; Deuteronomy 32:8; 2 Samuel 22:14; Psalm 7:17; 9:2; 21:7; 46:4; 47:2; 50:14; Mark 5:7; Luke 8:28; Acts 7:48; 16:17; Hebrews 7:1). There is no one or nothing greater than God.

- **Lord -** (Genesis 15:7). God revealed himself as Lord throughout the books of Exodus, Leviticus, Numbers and Deuteronomy and throughout the Old and New Testaments (See John 20:28). One day, every knee will bow, and every tongue will confess that Jesus Christ is Lord. (Isaiah 45:23-25; Romans 14:11-13; Philippians 2:9-11)

- **Just and righteous judge -** Psalm 103:6 says, "The Lord executeth righteousness and judgment for all that are oppressed." Other scriptures are: (Psalm 103:17; 106:3-31; 111:3; 112:3-9; 119:142-144; 172; 143:1-12)
  - Because He is just and righteous, there are some things that He hates. "These six things doth the Lord hate: yea, seven are an abomination unto him. A proud look, a lying tongue, and hands that shed innocent blood, An heart that deviseth wicked imaginations, feet that be swift in running to mischief, A false witness that speaketh lies, and he that soweth discord among brethren." (Proverbs 6:16-19(KJV) "And I saw heaven opened, and behold a white horse; and he that sat upon him was called Faithful and True, and in righteousness he doth judge and make war." (Revelation 19:11)

13

- Because God is righteous, sin had to be paid for, and mankind had to be redeemed. We could not redeem ourselves. Jesus paid the price for us and settled the sin debt for us all. God has delivered us from the power of darkness and has translated us into the kingdom of his dear Son. (Colossians 1:12-14)

- **Alpha and Omega** – the beginning and the end, the first and the last. (Revelation 1:8-11; Revelation 21:6-8). God is everlasting. (Isaiah 9:6-7; 26:4; 40:28-31; 63:16; Psalm 145:13)

- **Our shepherd and the door of the sheep -** (Psalm 23; John 10:7-11). See more information in Chapter 2 on the role of a shepherd.

- **Our provider - Jehovah-Jireh** – (Genesis 22:13-14). God meets our needs.

- **Our shield -** (Deuteronomy 33:29; Psalm 3:3; 28:7; 33:20; 59:11; 84:9-11; 91:4; 115:9-11; 119:114; 144:2; Proverbs 30:5) and our exceeding great reward (Genesis 15:1)

- **Our banner – Jehovah Nissi -** (Exodus 17:15) God is the protector, leader, and deliverer of His people. He exhibited this for the Israelites. He is willing and able to do the same thing for us today.

- **Our peace – Jehovah Shalom -** (Judges 6:23-24; John 14:27; Ephesians 2:14). God is not the author of confusion. He is the God of peace. (1 Corinthians 14:33)

- **Our righteousness** – (Jeremiah 23:6; and 33:16; Job 36:3; Matthew 6:33; Romans 1:17; 3:21-25; 10:3; 2 Peter 1:1). Jesus is our righteousness. Because he has paid the price for our sin, we are righteous; not because we do everything right, but because when we accept Jesus into our heart, God declares us righteous.

- **Our rock** - God is strong, steadfast and stable. (Deuteronomy 32:4; 1 Samuel 2:2; 2 Samuel 22:3; 22:32-33; 22:47; 23:3; Psalm 18:2; 18:31; 18:46; 42:9; 62:7; 78:35; 89:26; 94:22; Isaiah 17:10). He is a solid foundation that we can build our faith on.

- **Our strong tower** - (Psalm 61:3; Proverbs 18:10). We can run to God and find safety in Him.

- **Our healer – Jehovah Rapha** - God revealed himself as a healer in the Old and New Testaments. (Some examples are: Exodus 15:26; Psalm 107:20; Isaiah 53:1-5; Hosea 11:3; Matthew 4:24; 12:15; 14:14; 15:30; Mark 6:5-13; Luke 4:40-41; 6:17-18; 8:26-36; 9:11; 13:14; 17:11-16; John 4:46-54; 1 Peter 2:20-25.)

- **King of Kings and Lord of Lords** – (1 Timothy 6:15; Revelation 17:14 and 19:16). God is greater than all things, people, spirits, and powers.

- **God is wise – He is the only wise God** - (1 Timothy 1:17; Jude 1:25) He uses the foolishness of this world to confound the wise (1 Corinthians 1:17-29). "For my thoughts are not your thoughts, neither are your ways my ways, saith the Lord. For as the heavens are higher than the earth, so are my ways higher than your ways, and my thoughts than your thoughts."(Isaiah 55:8-9). The wisdom of the world is foolishness with God. (1 Corinthians 3:19-20).

- **God is truth - God cannot lie** - (Numbers 23:19). I often hear people talking about "speaking their own truth." I believe we can share our experiences and have our perspectives, but God is the standard for truth. Think of measurements. If everyone had a different "truth" about how long a foot is or how many ounces equals a pound, you would have chaos. If one person said an ordinary dime was worth ten cents and another person said it was worth a dollar and yet another said it was worth one cent, you would have a hard time determining the cost of an item. Just as there have to be set standards for measurements, it's even more important for there to be a reliable standard for the truth. God sets the standards for truth because He is truth.

- **God is gracious and rich in mercy -** (Exodus 34:5-7; 2 Chronicles 30:1-9; Nehemiah 9; Psalm 103:8-17; 111:4; 118;136; 145:8; Isaiah 30:19; 54:7-8; 55:7; Joel 2:13; Jonah 4:2; Malachi 1:9: Ephesians 2:4-7). Even when we were dead in sins, God sent Jesus to save us. His mercies are new every morning (Lamentations 3:22-23).

- **A restorer** -- God can restore what has been lost (Joel 2:23-32).

- **A rewarder** – When we come to God, we must believe that He is who He says He is, and "that he is a rewarder of them that diligently seek him." (Hebrews 11:6)

- **The Father, Son, and the Holy Spirit/Holy Ghost are one** - "For there are three that bear record in heaven, the Father, the Word, and the Holy Ghost: and these three are one." (1 John 5:7) Although not mentioned specifically in Genesis, we learn that **Jesus and the Holy Spirit were also a part of the creation.**

  - **The Word** – "In the beginning was the Word, and the Word was with God, and the Word was God. The same was in the beginning with God. All things were made by him; and without him was not any thing made that was made. In him was life; and the life was the light of men. And the light shineth in darkness; and the darkness comprehended it not." (John 1:1-5). "And the Word was made flesh, and dwelt among us, (and we beheld his glory, the glory as of the only begotten of the Father,) full of grace and truth." (John 1:14) "For the Word of God is quick, and powerful, and sharper than any two-edged sword, piercing even to the dividing asunder of soul and spirit, and of the joints and marrow, and is a discerner of the thoughts and intents of the heart." (Hebrews 4:12). All scripture is given by inspiration of God (2 Timothy 3:16-17).

  - **Jesus is one with the Father** (John 10:30). **Jesus is the visible image of the invisible God.** (Colossians 1:10-17). Jesus said, "If you have seen me, you have seen the Father." (John 14:9-12; Colossians 1:15-16). Jesus is the same yesterday, today, and forever (Hebrews 13:8).

- o **God is a spirit,** and we must worship him in spirit and in truth. (John 4:24)

- **The Holy Spirit/Holy Ghost:**
  - o Was a part of creation. "In the beginning God created the heaven and the earth. And the earth was without form, and void, and darkness was upon the face of the deep. And the **Spirit** of God moved upon the face of the waters." (Genesis 1:1-2)
  - o **Jesus is the child of Mary and the Holy Ghost (Matthew 1:18-21).** Jesus referred to himself as the Son of man and the Son of God (Matthew, Mark, Luke and John). He was both human and divine.
  - o Jesus baptizes with the Holy Ghost and with fire. (Matthew 3:11 & Luke 3:16)
  - o Led Jesus into the wilderness to be tempted of the devil (Matthew 4:1; Luke 4:1-2). I believe He knew that Jesus would overcome the devil.
  - o Our heavenly Father will give the Holy Spirit to those that ask Him. (Luke 11:13)
  - o Revealed in different shapes: a **dove** (Matthew 3:16; Mark 1:10; Luke 3:16-22; John 1:32); **a mighty rushing wind & cloven tongues of fire** (Acts 2:1-4)
  - o The Holy Ghost **gives power**: (Luke 24:49; Acts 1:8)

- The Holy Spirit is a Teacher, Comforter, and Spirit of Truth (Luke 12:12; John 14:15-26; 15:26-27; John 16:7-13; 1 Corinthians 2:13)
- Gives gifts (Hebrews 2:4)
- Makes intercession for us according to the will of God (Romans 8:26-27).
- Fruit of the Spirit is: love, joy, peace, longsuffering, gentleness, goodness, faith, meekness, and temperance. (Galatians 5:22-23; Ephesians 5:9-10). I recommend that you also read these verses in the Message Bible or the Amplified Bible.
- Praying in the Holy Ghost builds you up. (Jude 1:20)
- Seals us and is the "earnest" – down payment – of our inheritance and dwells in us. (Romans 8:9; 1 Corinthians 6:19; Ephesians 1:2-14). Our body is the temple of the Holy Spirit, and we shouldn't grieve Him. (Ephesians 4:29-32; Ephesians 5:1-33)
- The only sin that will not be forgiven is blasphemy against the Holy Ghost. (Matthew 12:31-32)
- Jesus had to go so that the Holy Spirit could come (John 16:7)
- Reproves/Convicts the world of sin, righteousness, and judgment. (John 16:7-11)
- Glorifies Jesus (John 16:14)
- Gives life (2 Corinthians 3:1-6)

Chapter 2: Know Who You Are & How Precious You Are to God

- **God loves you and has provided a way to reconcile/redeem you to Himself.** (John 3:16; Ephesians 2:4-18; Ephesians 5:1-2; 1 John 4:10). **God created everything, including mankind. God is the owner of it all** – Psalm 24:1-2 NIV: "The earth is the Lord's and everything in it, the world and all who live in it; for he founded it on the seas and established it on the waters." Heaven is God's throne and earth is His footstool (Isaiah 66:1; Matthew 5:34-35; Acts 7:49). The owner of the property determines who can legally enter it. God has made faith in Jesus Christ, the only entry point to Him. He wants all to come to Him, but **there is only one door in.**

  - **Jesus is the "door of the sheep" (**John 10:7-9). Read the parable that Jesus gave about the kingdom of heaven being like a king who made a marriage for his son and invited guests (Matthew 22: 1-10). The servants of the king brought rich, poor, Jew & Gentile, and different people of different races and stature. Each was given a wedding garment, but one man came to the wedding feast without the wedding garment. I believe having Jesus in your heart is the wedding garment. The King spotted the man and cast him out (Matthew 22:11-14**). Jesus said, "no man cometh unto the Father, but by me" (John 14:6)**. He knocks on the door but won't go in unless he's invited. He even knocks on the door of the lukewarm church. *"Behold, I stand at the door, and knock: if any man hear my voice, and open the door, I will come in to him, and will sup with him, and he with me."* (Revelation 3:20) This verse was written to the church of the Laodiceans.

- **Because of His love, God sent Jesus to save us and not to condemn us.** (John 3:16-21; Galatians 4:1-9)

- **Jesus is the only way to the Father.** Jesus said, *"I am the way, the truth, and the life: no man cometh unto the Father, but by me."* (John 14:6) Not everyone that says Lord, Lord will enter the kingdom of heaven… (Matthew 7: 21-23) You must be born again. (John 3:3-7 & 1 Peter 1:22-23)

- **God is not willing that any should perish**, but that all should come to repentance (2 Peter 3:8-10). Why then do people perish? (Read Matthew 25:41-46 and you will find out that hell was not prepared for mankind but for the devil and his angels.) Hell hath enlarged herself (Isaiah 5:13-14). Accepting Jesus into your heart allows you entry to heaven. If we perish, it is because we did not choose to accept God's gift of salvation – Jesus Christ.

- **Truth** – Jesus is the way, the truth and the life…. (John 14:6; John 8:31-32). Jesus said to those Jews who had believed Him, "If you continue in my word, then you are truly disciples of mine; and you will know the truth, **and the truth shall make you free."**

- o **Jesus came that we might have life and have it more abundantly** (John 10:10; 1 Corinthians 2:9 and Ephesians 3:20).

- o **We are saved by grace through faith in Jesus Christ.** (Ephesians 2:8 -9). We can't work our way to heaven. When we do good work, we should do it because we love Him (if ye love me, keep my commandments (John 14:15-21). Know that His grace is sufficient. (2 Corinthian 12:9) <u>**We can't earn salvation. We can't buy happiness nor contentment**</u> -- not even if you had all the money, fame, or friends in the world. What profits a man to gain the whole world and lose his own soul...? (Mark 8:36-37). I need to say again: We are saved by grace through faith in Jesus Christ.

- o **Nothing can separate us from the love of God** (Romans 8:35-39). God is the one who justifies us.

- o **God has given us gifts.** Jesus gave gifts to men when he ascended to heaven (Ephesians 4:8). "But we have this treasure in earthen vessels, that the excellency of the power may be of god, and not of us." (2 Corinthians 4:7)

- **He made you an heir** (Galatians 4: 6-8; 1 Peter 1:3-5**).** Never forget that you are who God says you are. He determines your identity, your value and your worth. If you've accepted Jesus Christ, then you are a child of the Most High God; an Heir of God and joint heir with Jesus Christ; a recipient of an inheritance. **YOU** are in Christ's will. You are the righteousness of God in Christ Jesus. (2 Corinthians 5:19-21)

- o You may question being made the righteousness of God. Vs. 21 states: "For he hath made him to be sin for us, who knew no sin; that we might be made the righteousness of God in him." Years ago, while studying an insurance course, I learned the terms vicarious liability and imputed liability. The concept is a legal doctrine that assigns liability for an injury to a person who did not cause the injury but who had a legal relationship with the person who did. Examples could include: parents of minor children could be vicariously liable for their child's actions; employers could be liable for employee actions; a getaway driver could be liable for the murder of the person that his cohort killed in the commission of a crime.
- o God made Jesus vicariously liable for the sins of the whole world (Galatians 1:4; 1 John 2:2). He took on the liability and paid the debt for all of our sins. God then imputed righteousness to us through Jesus Christ. We are righteous because God says we are righteous.
- o Heirs to an inheritance must claim the inheritance and meet the conditions in the will in order to obtain their inheritance. Salvation is the inheritance, and the conditions are: being

saved by grace through faith in Jesus Christ, confessing with your mouth the Lord Jesus and believing in your heart that God raised him from the dead (Romans 3:21-26; 10:8-11, Ephesians 2:4-10). **THE GOOD NEWS** is: Jesus has paid the penalty for sin through his shed blood. He wants us to believe him and to receive him. **It's your choice whether or not you claim the benefits of the will or you reject and forfeit the gift of your inheritance. Only you can make this choice. Others can't make it for you. Choose wisely.**

- **God has a good plan for you**. His plan is for good and not evil. (Jeremiah 29:11 KJV) "For I know the thoughts that I have toward you, saith the Lord, thoughts of peace, and not of evil, to give you an expected end." "I know what I'm doing. I have it all planned out— plans to take care of you, not abandon you, plans to give you the future you hope for. (Jeremiah 29:11 – The Message Bible). You are not a mistake. God knew you before you were formed in the womb (Jeremiah 1:5). "For we are his workmanship, created in Christ Jesus unto good works, which God hath before ordained that we should walk in them. (Ephesians 2:10)

  - God's gifts are without repentance (Rom 11:29). You may see some people with incredible talents and gifts but who are not living a godly life. I believe that God gives everyone a gift, a talent, and a purpose. It's up to you to use it for what it was intended, bury it, or use it unwisely. It's your choice.

- o God wants us to prosper. Some examples: Joseph prospered and had favor even while he was a slave and a prisoner (Genesis 39:3-23). Joshua prospered and had success (Joshua 1:7). The children of Israel won battles (2 Chronicles 20:20). Gaius (3 John 1:2). Keep God's words and do them that you may prosper (Deuteronomy 29:9).
- o God determines our value. He has numbered the hairs on our heads (Matthew 10:27-31; Luke 12:4-7). He knows us and knew us before we were born. In fact, he said to Jeremiah, "Before I formed you in the womb I knew you, before you were born I set you apart; I appointed you as a prophet to the nations." (Jeremiah 1:5 NIV). He is the shepherd and calls his sheep by name (John 10:1-3). In our society, we determine the value of an item by its usefulness and even by whose name is on the label. We just might have an invisible label that could say, "Created by Almighty God."

Chapter 3: Know That You Have an Enemy

- **You have an enemy called the devil, whose goal is to kill, steal, and destroy you.** (John 10:10) Your enemy is a murderer and a liar. (John 8:44) He will try to kill, steal and destroy your health, your joy, your friendships, your marriage, your family, your finances, your mind, your work, your identity, your reputation, your faith, your purpose, truth, the Word of God, and ultimately your life. He:
    - Walks about as a roaring lion, seeking whom he may devour (1 Peter 5:8)
    - Is a deceiver and is the antichrist (2 John 1:7)
    - Is a liar (1 John 2:22)
    - Is a murderer, liar, and the father of lies (John 8:44)
    - Is an accuser of the brethren (Revelation 12:10)
    - Is an enemy (Matthew 13:24-30)
    - Has great wrath/anger, because he knows he only has a short time on earth. (Revelation 12:12)
    - Will be destroyed along with the beast, the false prophet, and death (Hebrews 2:14-15; Revelation 19:20; 20:10-15)
- **The battle is about the word of God.** Attacks are designed to steal God's Word away from you to make you vulnerable to losing your faith and open to attacks. See the parable of the sower and the seed. (Matthew 13:1-21)

- **Fight the good fight of faith.** Remember, we don't wrestle against flesh and blood (Ephesians 6:12). We are in a spiritual war, and we must **put on the whole armor of God as we prepare to fight** (Ephesians 6:10-18). The weapons of our warfare are not carnal but mighty through God to the pulling down of strongholds. Jesus said He would never leave us nor forsake us (Hebrews 13:5), and he will always be with us even unto the end of the world (Matthew 28:20). **Fighting strategies:**
  - **Submit & resist** - James 4:7 tells us we are to submit to God, resist the devil and he will flee from us. If you are in rebellion to God and not submitting, the devil won't flee. Put things in the right order. Submit to God first, then resist the devil, and he will flee because God will cause him to flee.
  - **Praise** – God inhabits the praises of His people. When God is there, deliverance comes (Psalm 22:3-5). Praise is powerful and can be a weapon to confuse the enemy
  - **Fasting, prayer, praise, and joy are weapons** (Isaiah 58:6-14; Matthew 17:20-21 & Mark 9:29). Fasting and prayer work with praise: 2 Chronicles 20 tells of a battle between King Jehoshaphat and the Ammonites and Moabites. Jehoshaphat and the inhabitants of Judah were outnumbered, so Jehoshaphat called for a fast and sought God in prayer. The Israelites received a word from God that told them they would be delivered from the enemy. They wouldn't even need to fight because God would deliver them.

The next day the king appointed singers unto the Lord to praise God and when they began to sing, God set ambushes against the Ammonites and Moabites. The Ammonites and Moabites killed each other, and the people of Judah did not need to fight at all. Nehemiah tells us that the joy of the Lord is our strength (Nehemiah 8:10).

- **Please God** – "When a man's ways please the Lord, he maketh even his enemies to be at peace with him." (Proverbs 16:7)   It is impossible to please God without faith. (Hebrews 11:6)
- **Fight with words:**
  - Speak what God speaks to you and about you and your circumstances. "For by thy words thou shalt be justified, and by thy words thou shalt be condemned" (Matthew 12:37). And when you pray, **say…**(Luke 11:2). Don't just think it, SAY IT.
  - Your response in a situation may either help to deter a fight or cause a fight. "A soft answer turns away wrath: but grievous words stir up anger." (Proverbs 15:1)
  - Jesus quoted the word when he was tempted (Matthew 4:1-11)
  - The sword of the Spirit is the Word of God (Ephesians 6:17). The Word of God is your weapon. Learn to use it.

Chapter 4: Know That You Will Face Challenges in Life

- **Some challenges may be physical, others mental, and some spiritual.** One of the greatest battles will take place in your mind – how you see things and what you dwell on. It can influence how you think, feel, believe, as well as how you see and treat yourself and others. Instead of dwelling on bad thoughts, think on things that are honest, just, pure, lovely of a good report, are virtuous and praiseworthy (Philippians 4:8). Control your thoughts, or they will control you and could lead to wrong thinking, feelings of fear, inferiority, low self-esteem, a lack of self-worth, or all types of sins.

  - **Everyone will face challenges at some point in life.** If people tell you that Christians are immune from challenges; that is a lie. The Bible says, "Many are the afflictions of the righteous but the Lord shall deliver them out of them all" (Psalm 34:19). Jesus said: "The servant is not greater than his master" ... If they have persecuted me, they will also persecute you; if they have kept my saying, they will keep yours also." (John 13:16 and 15:20-21). Challenges are temporary. I wish I could, but I can't tell you how long each challenge, test, or trial will last. **At some point in time, they will end.** Suffering can be tough and can cause great despair (2 Corinthians 1:8-11), but God promised to never leave us nor forsake us.

- Temptations will come (James 1:2-4). You don't have to yield to them; but, if you do yield, repent, confess it as sin and move on. Call sin what it is. That's part of the confession. When we do, God is faithful and just to forgive us of our sin and to cleanse us from all unrighteousness (1 John 1:8-9).

- The Bible says the temptations you face are "common to man: but God is faithful, who will not suffer you to be tempted above that ye are able, but will with the temptation also make a way of escape, that you may be able to bear it." (1 Corinthian 10:13) The key here is that you are not the only one facing whatever temptation you are going through. James 1: 12-15 tells where temptations come from. It doesn't come from God. Read these verses in the Message Bible.

- God is able to work all things together for good to those that love Him and are "the" called according to his purpose (Romans 8:28-29). This is a mystery; but somehow, God in His wisdom and power can cause all things to work together for good to them that love Him and are the called according to His purpose. He is better than a navigation system. He even knows how to use your mistakes to get you to the needed destination.

- Be wise and build on a solid foundation – the rock is Jesus Christ. (Matthew 7:24-27). When you build on a solid foundation, you will be able to withstand the winds and storms the enemy sends your way.

- o **At some point, you will lose someone you love. Our bodies will die, but our spirits live on for eternity in heaven or in hell.**
  - **Death began with sin** – when Adam & Eve ate of the tree of knowledge of good and evil that the Lord had commanded him not to eat (Genesis 2:15-17). Something happened at that point that caused the body to be susceptible to sickness, disease, injury, and all the ramifications of sin. It will end when death is cast into the lake of fire. Death is described as the last enemy (1 Corinthians 15:26; Revelation 20:14).
  - **It is appointed unto men once to die, but after this the judgment.** (Hebrews 9:27-28; 2 Corinthians 5:10)
  - **If you are in Christ, to be absent from the body is to be present with the Lord.** (2 Corinthians 5:1-11)
  - **Read Luke 16:19-31 the story of the rich man and Lazarus and their deaths.** One went to hell and could see Lazarus in Abraham's bosom.
  - **God wants us to seek him--not the dead.** Don't try to contact the dead through witches, wizards, mediums, tarot cards, séances, Ouija boards, etc.

31

(Leviticus 19:31; 20:5-6; Deuteronomy 18:10-11; 1 Samuel 28; 2 Kings 21:6-15; 23:24-26; Isaiah 8:17-20). If you need wisdom, ask God. (James 1:5)

- **Find comfort in knowing that when Jesus returns, the dead in Christ will rise first.** Then we which are alive and remain shall be caught up together with them in the clouds to meet the Lord in the air.... (1 Thessalonians 4:14-18)

- **Jesus understands what you are going through.**
  - In the garden of Gethsemane, Jesus told his disciples to watch and pray because **"the spirit is willing but the flesh is weak."** (Matthew 26:41 & Mark 14:38).
  - He is the high priest touched with the feeling of our infirmities because **he was tempted i**n every manner like us, **yet without sin** (Hebrews 4:15).
  - He is the great high priest who **makes intercession for us** (Romans 8:34). Jesus prayed for Peter, and he prays for us. (Luke 22:31-32)
  - Jesus was sinless but **suffered and died** for our sins (Hebrews 5:8; 1 Peter 2:21-25). Jesus **had scars** (nail prints in his hands and a pierced side). We may carry scars from things that have happened to us, but Jesus understands that as well. (John 20:19-29)
  - Jesus **died and rose** from the dead. (Romans 14:9; 2 Corinthians 5:15; 1 Thessalonians 4:14)

- He was **despised and rejected** of men; a man of sorrow and acquainted with grief (Isaiah 53:3). Jesus was rejected **(not received)** by his own people (John 1:10-11) -- the very ones who were looking for the Messiah to come.
- Jesus said, "foxes have holes, and the birds of the air have nests; but the Son of man **hath not where to lay his head**." (Matthew 8:20 & Luke 9:58 KJV)

- **Beware of the lust of the flesh, the lust of the eyes and the pride of life** (1 John 2:15-17). Not everything that's good to you is good for you. Not everything that feels good or tastes good is good. Your flesh will crave for things it doesn't need. What you see with your eyes can cause you to lust (Matthew 5:28). Pride comes before destruction (Proverbs 16:18).

- **Beware of imposters. They come as:**
  - Wolves in sheep's clothing (Matthew 7:15-16). Things and people are not always what they pretend to be. Beware of wolves in sheep's clothing. Remember the story of Little Red Riding Hood and the Big Bad Wolf. He pretended to be her grandmother by dressing like her, but he was really a wolf. The only thing he wanted to do was trick her so that he could kill her and eat her. Wolves will eventually show you their fangs, but it may take a while. If you get a "bad feeling" about something or someone, don't ignore it. It could be God warning you that something isn't right. Don't let your guard down. Some people will pretend to be your friend, but they are wolves...only wanting

what they can get or take from you. Many will say Lord Lord (Matthew 7:22-23), but Jesus will say, *"I never knew you: depart from me, ye that work iniquity."* Jesus knows the wolves from the sheep. Sometimes we can't always tell the difference, but Jesus can.

o   False prophets (Matthew 7:15-23 and Chapter 24:23-25); Jesus warned about false prophets who will even show great signs and wonders, insomuch that, if it were possible, they shall deceive the very elect. He said we would know them by their fruit.

o   Satan transforms as an angel of light (2 Corinthians 11:14-15). Not everyone who proclaims to be a Christian is one, and not all people who profess Christ have been transformed. We may not be able to distinguish them, but God can. (Matthew 7:15-27; 25:1-46; Luke 13:23-30). This can also refer to some in the ministry; not all who claim to be saved are saved. (Matthew 7:21-23)

Chapter 5: Know That No One Is Perfect

- **No one is perfect.** Despite what you may hear or what people will lead you to believe, no one on Earth is perfect. (Mark 10:18 – no one is good but the Father). If you expect perfection in everything, you will be disappointed. Besides, you aren't perfect either. Be willing to forgive because we all make mistakes. For all have sinned and fall short of the glory of God (Romans 3:23).

- **People will fail us** because they are human. **Peter denied Jesus** (Mark 14:66-72); **Judas betrayed Jesus** (Mark 14:10; Luke 22:3-4; 47-48); **the disciples denied him and ran away** (Mark 14:50). Your ultimate trust should be in God, not man. Trust no man – we shouldn't trust people to the same extent we trust God. People will fail us because they are imperfect. (Psalm 146:3-5; 118:8; Micah 7:5-7)

- **There may even be times when you will fail yourself.** We can be just as disappointed with ourselves as we are with other people. Confess your faults, (James 5:16); however, choose wisely who you confess to. Don't confess to a tattletale, busybody, or gossiper (1 Timothy 5:13). If you fall or fail God, yourself, or others, ask for and receive forgiveness; and then move on. Even the apostle Paul was frustrated with himself (Romans 7:8-24).

- **You can't fix everything, but you can pray about everything and turn everything over to God.** Pray without ceasing (1 Thessalonians 5:17). Cast your cares upon Jesus (1

Peter 5:7 & Matthew 11:28-30). With men, things are impossible, but with God, all things are possible (Matthew 19:26).

- **God is your source**. The government is not your source. Your job is not your source. Money is not your source. Your family is not your source. The government is flawed because it is made up of flawed people. People are not perfect. Not every law lines up with the Word of God. God may use laws, jobs, money, or people as resources, but these things do not limit Him. The Earth belongs to God. (Psalm 24:1-2; 1 Corinthians 10:26). He can do more than we can ask or think (Ephesians 3:20). He even used ravens to feed the prophet, Elijah. (1 Kings 17:3-6)

- **We walk by faith, not by sight** (2 Corinthians 5:6-7). Just because you can't see something with your eyes, doesn't mean it's not real. You can't see the wind, germs, viruses, bacteria, or spirits – but they exist (Romans 1:20; 2 Corinthians 4:18). For years people wondered what caused sickness and disease. When the microscope was invented, they discovered germs and bacteria, the atom, protons, and neutrons. We are still discovering more about things that are invisible to the eye. Some people say, "I won't believe it unless I see it." Well, you won't see everything. There are things you have to accept by faith. Faith is the substance of things hoped for the evidence of things not seen (Hebrews 11:1).

- **You will find God when you seek Him with all your heart** (Deuteronomy 4:29). It is so easy to get distracted, especially when praying and studying. Just keep pressing through. Get past the distractions. Pray, seek, study, praise, and listen.

- **We are hid in Christ** (Colossians 3:1-3). When we are in Christ, God sees us through the shed blood of Jesus Christ. So he doesn't deal with us as sinners but as sons and daughters. So let's set our affections on things above.

Chapter 6: Know The Value Of What You Have And The Cost To Acquire It.

- **Your body is the temple of the Holy Spirit** (1 Corinthians 6:19). Treat it like one.

- **Your soul is valuable.** Jesus asked, what profits a man to gain the whole world and lose his own soul (Matthew 16:26; Mark 8:36; Luke 9:25). We are living souls filled with the very breath of God. (Genesis 2:7) God wants our souls to prosper (3 John 1:2)
  - Your soul is so valuable **that God sent His only begotten Son to die for you.** (John 3:16). God doesn't want anyone to perish, He wants everyone to repent (2 Peter 3:9).
  - **God knows your name and has good plans for you.** (Exodus 33:12-17; John 10:3; Jeremiah 29:11)

- **The grass isn't always greener on the other side** – see the story of the prodigal son. He thought his life would be better if he received his portion of his inheritance from his father. His father gave him what he wanted, but the prodigal son wasted his money, lost his friends, and ended up feeding pigs. (Read Luke 15:11-32). A few years ago, I heard about the 80/20 principle in relationships. Someone may have 80% of what they need and want in a relationship but may leave that relationship to pursue the 20% they wish they had. They later learn that although they gained the 20%, they were looking for, they are now missing the 80% of what they previously had. We must learn to appreciate what we have and not give it up while looking for something that will be far less satisfactory in the long run. Know the value of what you have. Many have sold valuable items in garage sales only to find out later that the items were worth millions. Jesus gave two parables related to this: the parable of the treasure hidden in a field and a parable of a merchant seeking good pearls (Matthew 13:44-46). When the men found each item, they sold all that they had to buy the field and the pearl because they understood their value.

- **We have a new covenant with God through Jesus Christ** (Hebrews 8:8-13; 10:16-17 and 12:24). This new covenant is written by God in our hearts and minds. God will not remember our sins and iniquities anymore.

Because of Jesus, we have great value. So, stop wearing the labels other people put on you; instead, wear these designer labels of how I believe God sees you (<u>underlined</u> words are for males, and *italicized* words are for females). I encourage you to confess these words over yourself. I call them: God's Designer Labels.

GOD'S DESIGNER LABELS
YOU ARE:

A champion + A child of the Most High God + A forgiver + A good listener + Accepted + Adventurous + An achiever + Anointed + Approved + Articulate + Beautiful + Blessed + Bold + Brave + Caring + <u>Chivalrous</u> + Chosen + Confident + Considerate + Delivered + Disciplined + Effective + *Elegant* + Eloquent + Empathetic + Energetic + Established + Faithful + Favored + Fearless + *Feminine* + Flexible + Focused + Forgiven + Free + Friendly + Fruitful + Full of life + Full of potential + Fun + <u>Gallant</u> + Generous + Genuine + Gifted + God's Masterpiece + *Gorgeous* + Gracious + Grateful + Grounded + <u>Handsome</u> + Healed + Healthy + Helpful + Highly favored + Honest + Humble + Insightful + Inventive + Joyful + Jubilant + Just + Justified + Keen + Kind + Knowledgeable + Leader + Loveable + Loved + Loving + <u>Masculine</u> + Marvelous + Memorable + Mighty + Miraculous + Musically Gifted + Neat + Needed + Nice + Noble + Obedient + Objective + Observant + Outstanding + Overcomer + Peaceful + Powerful + Prayerful + *Pretty* + Priceless + <u>Prince</u> + *Princess* + Productive + Protected + Qualified + Quick + Real + Redeemed + Repentant + Resilient + Resourceful + Righteous + Royalty + Safe + Saved + Secure + Self-controlled + Smart + Special + Strong + Successful + Sympathetic + Talented + Taken care of + Trusting in God + Trustworthy + Truthful + Unsurpassed + Upbeat + Uplifting + Upright + Useable by God + Useful + Valuable +

Victorious + Vindicated + Wanted + Whole – nothing missing and nothing broken + Worthy + Xenial + Xenodochial +"X-tra" Special + Yielded to God + Youthful + Zealous + Zesty

Jot down your key learnings from Part I:

_____

_____

_____

_____

_____

_____

_____

_____

_____

_____

_____

_____

_____

_____

_____

_____

_____

_____

_____

_____

_____

_____

_____

_____

My questions from Part I:

_____

_____

_____

_____

_____

_____

_____

_____

_____

_____

_____

_____

_____

_____

PART II: What I Hope You Will BE

Chapter 7: Be Like Christ

Jesus is our example. Jesus was and is:

- **Prayerful** - Jesus went off into a solitary place to pray; he prayed early in the morning (Matthew 14:23; Mark 1:35 & Luke 5:16); he prayed in the Garden of Gethsemane before he was arrested (Matthew 26:36-44 & Luke 22:39-46).
  - Thankful – Jesus expressed thanks to God. (Matthew 11:25; Luke 10:21; John 11:41). We should count our blessings, give thanks and be grateful for what we have. "In every thing give thanks: for this is the will of God in Christ Jesus concerning you." (1 Thessalonians 5:18)
  - Intercessor – Jesus prayed for Peter (Luke 22:31-32) and his disciples (John 17). He sits at the right hand of the Father, making intercession for us (Romans 8:34).
  - Prayed for the forgiveness of his enemies while they were crucifying him (Luke 23:33-34).
- **A mediator** (Hebrews 8:6) of a better covenant. He is an **advocate for us** with the Father (1 John 2:1-2).
- **Merciful** – Jesus showed mercy when the man cried, Jesus son of David have mercy on me (Luke 18:13-14 & Romans 9:15). Also, see God's mercy on page 16.
- **Filled with the Holy Ghost and was led by the Spirit** (Luke 4:1).

- o Told his disciples to receive the Holy Ghost (John 20:22 &
  Acts 1:4-8)
- o Jesus was anointed with the Holy Ghost and with power
  (Acts 10:38)
- **All Powerful** –Jesus said, "All power is given unto me in heaven
  and in earth." (Matthew 28:18)
- **Compassionate**– Jesus was moved with compassion toward the
  great multitude, and he healed their sick (Matthew 14:14; Mark 1:41;
  5:19; 6:34; 8:2). His compassion led to healing, raising the dead,
  feeding the hungry, casting out devils, etc. (Micah 7:19; Matthew
  8:16; 9:36; 15:32; 20:34; Romans 9:15); healing the blind (Luke 7:13-
  15)
- **Full of grace and truth** (John 1:14-17). Jesus did not condemn
  people, nor did he excuse or accept sin. He perfectly displayed
  grace & truth (John 3:17, 8:11 & 12:47). Jesus came to call sinners
  to repentance (Matthew 9:13; Mark 2:38; Luke 5:32). We also need
  to balance grace and truth. They go hand in hand. He didn't
  condemn the woman caught in adultery, but he told her to "go and
  sin no more."

  He called sin "sin" (John 8:3-11). He told the woman at the well that
  the man she was living with was not her husband (John 4:16-18). He
  told the man who was sick of the palsy, your sins are forgiven you
  (Mark 2:9). I heard a sermon by Dr. James Merritt on this topic, and
  he made some excellent points. I recommend you research his
  website to find the sermon on this topic of grace and truth.

Jesus healed a man at the Pool of Bethesda who had an infirmity for 38 years. Later, while the man was in the temple, Jesus found him there and said this: "Behold, thou art made whole: sin no more, lest a worse thing come unto thee." (John 5:1-14) Jesus healed through grace but warned the man what could happen if he continued in sin.

- **A good steward (employer/employee)** – Jesus said that he had not lost anyone that God gave to him, except "the son of perdition"; i.e., Judas. (John 17:12 & 18:9). He completed his mission (John 19:30)! Be a good steward over what God has given to you.

   o **We don't all have the same talents, skills, and abilities**. Your job is to make the most of what you have. If you don't, you may lose it. (Read Matthew 25:14-30.)

- **Emotional: Jesus expressed different emotions.**

   o **Anger but not sinful**. Jesus said, *"My Father's house should be a house of prayer but you have made it a den of thieves."* (Matthew 21:12-13 & Ephesians 4:26-27). Jesus took action and expressed his anger when he saw what they were doing in the temple. It's ok to be angry, but don't let anger turn into sin. Don't let the sun go down on your wrath: neither give place to the devil. (Ephesians 4:26-27). Staying angry and dwelling on offenses can open the door to the enemy allowing him to use that anger and that offense to lead you further into sin.

- **Jesus wept** before he raised Lazarus from the dead (John 11:33-35; Luke 19:41-48 and John 11:35). There will be times when we will cry, and that's ok.
- **Sorrowful** – In the garden of Gethsemane, Jesus told his disciples that his soul was "exceeding sorrowful, even unto death" (Matthew 26:38; Mark 14:34). Jesus understands sorrows, temptations, and disappointments.
- **Cared for the children of Jerusalem** – He talked about wanting to gather them together as a hen that gathers her chickens under her wing. (Matthew 23:37 & Luke 13:34)

- **Rebuked things that didn't align with the word or the will of God. Jesus rebuked:**
  - Satan (Matthew 4:10),
  - a fever (Luke 4:38-39 & Mark 1:29-31);
  - demons and unclean spirits (Matthew 17:14-21; Mark 1:32-34; 5:1-15; Luke 4::40-41; 9:38-43).
  - the wind and the sea (Matthew 8:26; Mark 4:39; Luke 8:24).
  - Peter, when he tried to keep Jesus from fulfilling his purpose. (Matthew 16:20-23 & Mark 8:29-33).
  - a deaf & mute spirit (Matthew 17:14-21; Mark 9:25-27).
  - disciples (Matthew 19:14; Mark 10:14 & 16:14; Luke 9:54-55 and 18:16)

- **Law abiding**
  - Jesus paid his taxes. (Matthew 17:24-27)

- o *Behold I stand at the door and knock* (Revelation 3:20). Jesus doesn't intrude nor comes where he's not wanted. He knocks on the door of our heart and waits for us to let him in.
- o Jesus submitted to authority – even when it was unjust (John 18 & 19). Jesus allowed himself to be arrested, beaten, and crucified even when he had done no wrong and had the power to call angels to rescue him. (Matthew 26:47-56)
- **Jesus is Saviour and Lord.** We are not! However, we can point people to and lead them to Jesus. A few scripture references are: Luke 1:47; 2:11; John 4:42; 20:28; Acts 5:31;13:23; Ephesians 5;23;Philippians 3:20; 1 Timothy 1:1. We can tell people about Jesus, share His word with them, disciple them, but we are not Lord over them. Beware if people try to use the word of God to control you. Jesus wants us to obey him because we love him (John 14:15). **Salvation only comes through Jesus Christ. "Neither is there salvation in any other: for there is none other name under heaven given among men, whereby we must be saved." (Acts 4:10-12).**
- **Worked as a carpenter** (Mark 6:3). Jesus had an occupation.
- **Shepherd** – (Isaiah 40:11); healed the sick (Matthew thru John); didn't condemn but yet told people not to sin anymore (John 5:14 & 8:11); Sought the lost. The shepherd's role is found in Psalm 23. *The shepherd was responsible for*:
  - o *Feeding the sheep* – He makes me lie down in green pastures; thou preparest a table before me in the presence

of my enemies. Fed the hungry. (Matthew 14:13-21 & Mark 8:1-9)

- o *Watering the sheep* – He leads me beside still waters. Water is essential for life. Jesus said He is the living water. (John 4:10)
- o *Grooming & cleaning* – He restores my soul; thou anoints my head with oil. Jesus makes us clean – from the inside out.
- o *Shearing-* the wool and inspecting the sheep's skin to determine the condition of the skin and the cleanliness of the fleece. He looks for signs of trouble.
- o *Delivering lambs* – when the sheep are in labor, the shepherd helps to deliver the lambs. Jesus told Peter to feed the lambs and the sheep. (John 21:15-17)
- o *Leading, Watching and Protecting* – he goes before the sheep and calls them as he leads them to pasture. He watched over them to keep them safe from wolves, bears, lions, thieves and anything that would harm them. At night he brought them back to the fold and counted them as they passed under the rod. The shepherd had to be prepared to lay down his life for the sheep (John 10:11).
- o *Going after the lost and wandering sheep* (Luke 19:10) and being tender with the young and the feeble (Matthew 9:12-13; Mark 2:17). Jesus said he came to seek and save the lost (Luke 19:10). Isaiah said we should seek Him while He may be found. (Isaiah 55:6)

- **Lamb of God** – Jesus was both a shepherd and a lamb. John referred to him as "the lamb of God which taketh away the sin of the world" (John 1:29). Several references are made in Revelation of Jesus being the Lamb (Revelation 7:9-17; 12:11; 13:8; 14:1-4; 15:3; 17:14; 21:9-27; 22:1-3). He was the perfect sacrifice for all sins.

- **Clean** – Jesus said that the "prince of this world" had nothing in him (John 14:30). The washing of the water cleanses us by the Word (Ephesians 5:26). Just as you should be clean spiritually, you should also be clean physically.

- **A good friend** – listens, supports, tells the truth, spends time together, and shares secrets. Jesus explained the parables to his disciples. He revealed the Father and the Holy Spirit to them. He told them of his impending death. (Read Matthew thru John). He remained friends with the disciples even when he knew they would deny him (Matthew 26). He called them "friends" (John 15:14-15).

- **A good host** – Jesus said, "*I go to prepare a place for you…*" (John 14:1-4). It's wonderful to know that Jesus is preparing a place for his people. Revelation 21:2 talks about the "new" Jerusalem *prepared* as a bride adorned for her husband. A good host prepares their home for their guests and should be diligent to keep the home prepared for those who live there.

- **Obedient** - Jesus:
  - **Was obedient to God** (John 9:4)
  - **Did only what he saw the Father do** (John 5:19-20 & 8:28-29).

- o **Submitted to his parents** (Luke 2:41-51)
- o **Submitted to the law and authority**. He paid his taxes, allowed himself to be brought before Pilate, and was crucified. Jesus set the example for us to follow. He did not allow the law to cause him to sin or deny the Father. "For the joy set before Him he endured the cross"……….(Hebrews 12:2)

- **A good child/sibling**
  - o Obeyed God and submitted to His will (Luke 22:42). He did only what he saw the Father do (John 5:19-36; 8:28; 8:49).
  - o Submitted to his earthly parents (Luke 2: 41-52).
  - o While hanging on the cross, he made provision for his mother (John 19:26-27).
  - o Jesus also had brothers and sisters (Matthew 1:25; 13:55-56; Mark 6:3; Luke 2:7; John 2:12).
  - o Spiritually, Jesus became the firstborn of many brethren (Romans 8:29 & Hebrews 2:17)

- **Faithful/Reliable** – He is faithful and will not leave us nor forsake us (Deuteronomy 31:6; Joshua 1:5; 1 Chronicles 28:20; Matthew 28:20; Hebrews 13:5).

- **Peaceful** – the giver of peace (John 14:27). When we need peace, ask Jesus for it and then receive it.

- **Truthful** – Jesus is the way the truth and the life (John 14:6; 18:37). God is not a man that He should lie (Numbers 23:19). We must speak the truth in love (Ephesians 4:15). It is impossible for God to lie (Hebrews 6:18).

- **Purposeful** – Jesus said, "I must needs go through Samaria." He was going there to meet the woman at the well who had been married multiple times and had a distorted view of worship (John 4:3-43). Many Samaritans were saved as a result of this. In another instance, Jesus waited until four days after Lazarus died before he went to visit. Jesus raised Lazarus from the dead to display the power of God. He doesn't always show up when we want him to, but his timing is always perfect and purposeful.

- **Overcomer of evil with the Word of God.** Jesus overcame temptations: study Matthew 4:1-11, KJV. When he was tempted in the wilderness, Jesus quoted the written word of God and did not yield to temptation. The temptation came to question Jesus' identity. Each temptation started with the phrase, "If thou be the Son of God."
  - When he was hungry and was told to command the stones to be made bread, Jesus said: *"It is written, Man shall not live by bread alone, but by every word that proceedeth out of the mouth of God."* We must know the word and know who we are in Christ. The Word of God is our sword (Ephesians 6:17; Hebrews 4:12).
  - When the devil tried to use the written word to cause Jesus to cast himself down from the pinnacle of the temple, the devil said, "for it is written, He shall give his angels charge concerning thee: and in their hands they shall bear thee up,

lest at any time thou dash thy foot against a stone." Jesus said: *"It is written again, Thou shalt not tempt the Lord thy God."* The verse in Psalm 91:11 reads: "For he shall give his angels charge over thee, <u>to keep thee in all thy ways.</u>" Jesus showed us that we must know the Word of God and know when it's quoted out of context or incompletely. The devil knows the word and will misquote it or quote it out of context to get people to fall. "Study to show thyself approved unto God, a workman that needeth not to be ashamed, rightly dividing the word of truth." (2 Timothy 2:15)

- When the devil told Jesus to bow down and worship him, Jesus said, *"thou shalt worship the Lord thy God and Him only shalt thou serve."*

- Jesus has overcome the world (John 16:32-33). We will overcome the accuser by the blood of the Lamb, and the word of our testimony (Revelation 12:11). Greater is he that is in us than he that is in the world (1 John 4:4). In Chapters 2 and 3 of the book of Revelation, Christ encourages the church to overcome.

- **The visible image of the invisible God** (Colossians 1:15**).** Jesus was the visible image of the invisible God. We are to let others see God in us. Be salt, be light, be a city set on a hill (Matthew 5:13-16).

- **Light of the world** – Jesus said that he is the light of the world and that if we follow him, we won't walk in darkness but will have the light of life (John 8:12 and John 1:9). Jesus said we are the salt of the earth and the light of the world; a city that is set on a hill. Let your light shine before people so that they may see your good works and glorify God (Matthew 5:13-16).

- **Persistent/Diligent/Finisher** – Jesus completes what he starts (Philippians 1:6 & Hebrews 2:2) ...."He that began a good work in you will complete it. He finished the assignment God gave him (John 4:34; 17:1-4; and John 19:30).

- **Jesus is the vine -** we are the branches. We must stay connected to him to continue to receive life and nourishment (John 15:1-11). Without him, we can do nothing (John 15:5)

- **Baptized** – Jesus allowed John the Baptist to baptize him. (Matthew 3:13-17). Jesus said in Mark 16:16: *"He that believeth and is baptized shall be saved; but he that believeth not shall be damned."* We are buried with Christ by baptism into his death, and just as he was raised up from the dead by the Father, we will also walk in newness of life (Romans 6:4; Colossians 2:12; Galatians 3:27). Jesus commanded his disciples to go and teach all nations and baptize them in the name of the Father, and of the Son, and of the Holy Ghost. **Have you been baptized yet? If you've accepted Jesus Christ, be sure to get baptized.**

- **The Word of God -** Jesus is the Word of God (John 1:1-5). Hide the word in your heart – memorize it (Psalm 119:11–12). Continue in the word, and you will know the truth, and it will make you free (John 8:32). The entrance of thy word brings light (Psalm 119:130).

- **A visionary** - where there is no vision the people perish (Proverbs 29:18). Jesus knew what his mission was and knew the outcome. He endured the suffering because he knew joy was coming... "who for the joy set before him endured the cross, despising the shame, and is set down at the right hand of the throne of God." (Hebrews 12:2)

- **A teacher** - Jesus taught the crowds by using parables, but he explained the meaning of the parables to his disciples (Matthew Chapters 5 thru 7; Mark 1:22; 2:13; 4:2; 10:1; Luke 4:31-32; John 8:2). Teach those close to you about what you have learned in life. Also, teach them the Word of God or get them in the right place so they can learn the Word. Jesus led by example and so should we.

- **Sacrificial** – Jesus became poor that we through his poverty might be made rich (2 Corinthians 8:9). Jesus became the sacrificial lamb. We have been redeemed by his blood and have obtained the forgiveness of sins (Ephesians 1:7; Colossians 1:14).

- **High Priest** - Jesus was a high priest who was tempted like we are tempted, but he did not sin (Hebrews 2:17; 4:15). He prays and intercedes for us (John 17:9-26; Romans 8:34).

- **Rested, slept, and He gives rest** – (Matthew 8:24-25; 11:27-30; Mark 4:38; Luke 8:23).

- **Got away from the crowds to spend time with the Father** (Mark 1:35) - We need to do the same.

- **Told us to "ask" in His name.** We should make our requests to God in Jesus' name (John 14:13-14; 15:16; 16:23-26).

- **Filled with wisdom -** "And the child grew, and waxed strong in spirit, filled with wisdom: and the grace of God was upon him." (Luke 2:40; Daniel 2:19-23; Romans 11:33; 1 Corinthians 1:17-31). It was important for Jesus to have the wisdom of God, and we need it as well. So ask God for wisdom (James 1:5).

- **Meek –** Jesus said the meek will inherit the earth (Matthew 5:5). Jesus is referred to as meek in Matthew 11:29 & 21:5. Today meek is defined as quiet, gentle, and easily imposed on; submissive. Moses was also called meek (Numbers 12:3). From these two examples, it is clear that you can be meek and powerful at the same time. I believe the key is being humble and submissive to God. Some Bible translations use the terms: mild, patient, longsuffering, gentle, kind, humble, and peaceful in place of the word, meek. Other scriptures referring "to the meek" include (Psalm 22:26; 25:9; 37:11; 76:9; 147:6; 149:4; Isaiah 11:4; 29:19; 61:1; & Zephaniah 2:3). All these references indicate how God favors the meek.

- **The righteous judge -** (Isaiah 2:1-4 & 2 Timothy 4:8). Jesus tells us in Matthew 7:1-6 not to judge because we can't see clearly enough to judge. We judge based on the outward appearance, but the Lord looks on the heart (1 Samuel 16:7). There are things we can't see and things we don't know. We can't see a person's heart. We may think we know their motive, but we can even be wrong about that too. Besides, we can't see clearly because of our imperfections, which is why Jesus in Matthew 7:1-5 says that we shouldn't judge (some versions say condemn).   The Message Bible (Matthew 7:1-2) reads: "Don't pick on people, jump on their failures, criticize their faults--unless, of course, you want the same treatment. That critical spirit has a way of boomeranging." We have things in our lives that prohibit us from seeing clearly; i.e., the beam or the mote in our own eyes. Jesus is the only one without sin. **We see things through our own filters.** Filters can be our backgrounds, our experiences, lack of experiences, our biases, prejudices, hurts, disappointments, etc. These things become the motes/beams in our eyes and cloud our ability to see. They influence our perspective and keep us from clearly seeing another person or accurately assessing a situation. God sees beyond all these things; that's why He is the righteous judge. **It's his job to judge, not ours. He alone determines who goes to heaven or hell** (Romans 10:6-11). It's ok to speak the truth, but do it in love.

- **God didn't send Jesus to condemn the world, but to save it.** Condemnation happens because people love darkness rather than light because their deeds are evil (John 3:16-21 & John 12:47-48). Jesus even says that we are not to judge according to the appearance but judge righteous judgement (John 7:24). Judgement will happen one day, but Jesus and his words will do the judging of those who reject him. (John 5:22-30; 12:46-50) Romans 2:16; 2 Timothy 4:1; Revelation 20:12-15)

- **Miracle worker and honors faith** – turned water to wine, fed the multitudes, healed the sick, cast out devils, and raised the dead (Matthew, Mark, Luke, and John). Jesus said that those who believe in him would do greater works (John 14:11-12).
- **Honors faith** – examples include (Matthew 8:5-16; 9:15-29; Mark 2:1- 12; 5:25-34; 10:46-52; Luke 7:2-10; 8:43-48; 17:12-19). It is impossible to please God without faith. (Hebrews 11:6)
- **Redeemer** – we have been redeemed with the precious blood of Christ (1 Peter 1:18-19)
    - **Jesus didn't come to call the righteous. He came to call sinners to repentance.** (Matthew 9:13; Mark 2:15-17; Luke 5:32)
- **Jesus overcame death and is risen from the dead. We serve a living God** (Matthew 17:9; 26:32; 28:6-7; Mark 14:28; 16:6-14; Luke 24:6-24; John 2:22; 21:14; Acts 3:15; 4:10; 13:30-34; Romans 2:24; 6:4-9; 7:4; 8:11; 10:9; Galatians 1:1; Ephesians 1:20; 1 Corinthians 15:20; 1 Thessalonians 1:10; 2 Timothy 2:8; 1 Peter 1:21). "Wherefore he saith, when he ascended up on high, he led captivity captive, and gave gifts unto men. (Now that he ascended, what is it but that he also descended first into the lower parts of the earth? He that descended is the same also that ascended up far above all heavens, that he might fill all things.") (Ephesians 4:8-10).

Jot down your key learnings from Part II:

_____

_____

_____

_____

_____

_____

_____

_____

_____

_____

_____

_____

_____

_____

_____

_____

_____

_____

_____

_____

_____

_____

_____

My questions from Part II:

_____

_____

_____

_____

_____

_____

_____

_____

_____

_____

_____

_____

PART III: Things I Hope You Will Do

Chapter 8: Love God

- **Love God with all your heart, mind, soul and strength.**
  (Deuteronomy 6:5; Matthew 22:37; Mark 12:30; Luke 10:27). Is it
  possible to love someone you don't know or don't know anything
  about? God commands us to love Him with all....so we must get to
  know Him.

  o We do this by learning about Him through His Word and
    prayer.

  o His Word communicates who God is.

  o **Study His Word** – it is a lamp that sheds light on who God is
    (2 Timothy 2:15 & Psalm 119:105). Read the Bible and ask
    God to reveal Himself to you.

  o **Communicate through prayer and meditate on the Word
    of God.** Talk to God and listen for Him to respond; usually
    this will happen through scripture.

  o **Obey him because you love him**. Jesus said, if you love
    me, keep my commandments (John 14:15). He doesn't want
    us to operate out of fear.

  o **Seek God.** You will find God when you seek Him with all
    your heart (Deuteronomy 4:29 & Jeremiah 29:13). Seek first
    the kingdom of God and his righteousness and you will have
    all the things you need (Matthew 6:25-34). In other words,
    seek the one who blesses and not the blessings. Arrange

your schedule around spending time with God, instead of fitting God into your schedule. God is a great provider.

- o **You must be "born again" by accepting Jesus into your heart.** (John 3:3-21 – read in the Message and Amplified Bibles; Romans 10:8-17) Believe with your heart and invite Him into your life as Lord and Saviour. Believing with your head is not good enough, even the devils believe in God. In fact, they know He exists, but they are in rebellion to Him. "Thou believest that there is one God; thou doest well: the devils also believe, and tremble." (Matthew 8:26-29). Faith without works is dead (James 2:17-26).

Chapter 9: Love Yourself

Jesus said, "love your neighbor as yourself" (Matthew 19:19). It's hard to love others when you don't love yourself. So here are some things I feel are essential as you go on this journey and learn to love yourself so that you can love others better.

- **Examine yourself.** When you love yourself, it's easier to love other people. Sometimes the things that irk us about other people are the things that we are doing ourselves. We may not be doing them to the same degree that they are, but our actions may be the same or similar. Example: have you ever been speeding 10 miles over the speed limit, but then someone passes you going a lot faster than you and you think or say something negative about them? Well, both of you are speeding. Just like with sin...whether a "big sin" or a "little sin"; it's all sin. Read Romans 2 and 2 Timothy 3:1-17 in the Message Bible.
  - **Examine yourself** (2 Corinthians 13:5 & 2 Peter 1:10-13) – are you in the faith of Jesus Christ? Also examine yourself before taking communion/the Lord's Supper (1 Corinthians 11: 23-33)
  - **Examine whether or not you are high minded/full of yourself?** (1Timothy 6:17-20; Romans 12:3-9)

- **Encourage yourself!**
  - o **Say what God says about you**. Speak positive words to yourself and about yourself!
    - ▪ Speak words of life (Proverbs 18:21; 17:27-28; 17:9; 18:8).
    - ▪ Speak the truth in love (Ephesians 4:15). Sometimes it's not what you say, but how you say it. If possible, speak the truth in a way that the other person can receive it.
    - ▪ Stir up the gifts of God that are in you. (2 Timothy 1:6)
  - o **Fight for yourself. You are worth fighting for.** When you love yourself you:
    - ▪ Take care of yourself because you value yourself.
    - ▪ Avoid things and people that will hurt you. Most people try or experiment with things because someone encouraged them to try it or called them "a chicken or a scared cat" for not trying it. We used to say, "I'd rather be a scared chicken than a dead duck." In other words, it's best not even to attempt to do some things that could lead to addiction or destruction; i.e., drugs, alcohol, pornography, witchcraft in all its various forms, sex outside of your marriage, etc.

- Being your best doesn't mean that you have to tear someone else down. We are all different for a reason. We could make a big difference in the world if each of us could be "our best selves."

o **When you hear the word of God nurture it and protect it.** Don't let the cares of this world, the deceitfulness of riches, and the lusts of other things enter in to choke the word and make it unfruitful in your life (Mark 4:18-19).

o **Recognize you are the only "you" in all the universe.** You are unique. This makes you special. You have a purpose. God has a plan for you. Be diligent and use your talents and gifts. "A man's gift makes room for him and brings him before great men." (Proverbs 18:16). Not everyone has the same talents. You will be accountable for how well you use the talents you've been given, not for how others use theirs (Matthew 25:14-46).

o **Be the best you possible.** You are your best when you are in Christ. When you love and don't hate, when you accept God's forgiveness, forgive others, when you receive God's love, and transform your mind. (Romans 12:1-2)

o **You must be born again in order to enter into the kingdom of God** (John 3:1-7 & Romans 10:1-17). Despite your background and your past, you can become new in Christ, and he will wipe your slate clean.

o **Be filled with the Holy Ghost** (John 20:21-22; Acts 2:38).

- **Trust God with all your heart and lean not to your own understanding** (Proverbs 3:5-8). There will be times when your faith is tested. There may even be times when it seems that God is silent or has turned His back on you. Hold on to your faith. Trust that He is faithful even when you may be going through rough times. The rough times will pass! I heard this point that resonated with me: while a teacher is preparing the class on a subject, the teacher is willing to answer all questions. However, on the day of the test, the teacher is not instructing and not talking but is assessing what the students have learned.
    - My mom used to sing this verse... "You can't hurry God, no you have to wait. You have to trust Him and give Him time, no matter how long it takes. He's a God that you can't hurry. He'll be there, don't you worry. Although He may not come when you want Him, He is always right on time." His ways are higher than our ways and his thoughts are higher than our thoughts. (Isaiah 55:9). No matter how much knowledge we gain, we will never be smarter than God.
    - Don't worry about tomorrow. God knows what you need. Make the most of today (Matthew 6:25-34).
- **Walk in faith--not in fear and not by sight** (2 Corinthians 5:7). God wants us to believe Him and to walk in faith. When He shows up, or He sends His angels, the word is always: "fear not." Faith and fear both involve "belief." Who will you believe?

- o **Believe what God says about you**. Don't have a grasshopper mentality. In other words, don't base your image of yourself on what others say about you or what you think about yourself. Believe that God can and will do what He says He will do. You will miss out on your blessing if you see yourself as a "grasshopper" and act on that belief rather than on what God says about you (Read Numbers chapters 13 and 14).
- o **Hope -** in the Bible means a strong and confident expectation (Romans 5:5). Faith is the substance of things hoped for the evidence of things not seen (Hebrews 11:1). Never give up hope.

- **Admit when you are wrong**. Make it your habit to confess your sins to one another and to pray for one another, so that you may be healed (James 5:16). The prayer of a righteous person is powerful and effective. Admit when you make a mistake, when you are wrong in an argument, or you do something unintentionally that hurts someone. Also, confess even when what you did was intentional. God doesn't want us running and hiding from Him. He already knows what you have done. He wants you to confess it and call it what it is. "If we confess *our sins*, he is faithful and just to forgive us our sins and to cleanse us from all unrighteousness." (1 John 1:9)

- **Tell the truth – be a person of integrity.** Do not bear false witness (Exodus 20:16: Proverbs 6:19; 12:17; 14:5; 17:4; 19:5-22; 21:28; Matthew 15:19; 19:18; Mark 10:19; Luke 18:20; Romans 13:9;

1 John 2:4; 4:20). Say what you mean: let your yes be yes and your no be no (Matthew 5:37).

- **Pray about everything.** There is nothing too small or too big to talk to God about. He cares about every aspect of your life. Pray for your loved ones, friends, job, enemies, leaders, wants, and needs. Also pray for those in authority (1 Timothy 2:1-6).
  - o **Prayers are powerful and are stored like incense in heaven** (Revelation 5:8).
  - o **Don't worry.** Cast your cares upon him because He cares for you (1 Peter 5:7).
  - o **Pray and give thanks** (Philippians 4:6).
  - o **Pray according to God's will.** "And this is the confidence that we have in him, that, if we ask anything according to his will, he heareth us. And if we know that he hear us, whatsoever we ask, we know that we have the petitions that we desired of him." (1 John 5:14-15)
  - o **Watch and pray that you don't fall into temptation** (Matthew 26:41; Mark 14:38)

- **Sing** – make a joyful noise unto the Lord. (Psalm 66:1; 81:1; 95:1-2; 98:4-6; 100:1) Instead of complaining, praise God and give thanks. Israel sent the singers out first in a battle, and the enemy became confused (2 Chronicles 20:1-28). Praise breaks chains: Paul & Silas sang in prison, and the prison doors opened, and their chains were loosed. There is power in praise (Acts 16:25-26). "But thou art holy, O thou that inhabitest the praises of Israel. Our fathers trusted in thee: they trusted, and thou didst deliver them. They cried unto thee, and were delivered: they trusted in thee, and were not confounded." (Psalm 22:3-5)

- **Keep/Guard/Protect your heart** (Proverbs 4:23), **your eyes** (Psalm 119:37; Proverbs 4:25-26), **your mouth** (Proverbs 4:24). Be mindful of what you say – the power of life and death is in the tongue (Proverbs 18:21). Guard your **ears.** "He that hath ears to hear, let him hear what the Spirit says to the churches." (Revelation 2:7-29: 3:6-22; 13:9). Be mindful of your **thoughts and what you dwell on**. Think about things that are true, honest, just, pure, lovely, of a good report, that are of virtue and praiseworthy (Philippians 4:8-9 KJV). This same verse in the Message Bible reads: "Summing it all up, friends, I'd say you'll do best by filling your minds and meditating on things true, noble, reputable, authentic, compelling, gracious—the best, not the worst; the beautiful, not the ugly; things to praise, not things to curse."
  - **You are what you believe in your heart.** (Proverbs 23:7 & Luke 6:45). The only way to change your heart is to renew your mind with God's word (Romans 12:2).
  - "Keep thy heart with all diligence, for out of it are the issues of life." (Proverbs 4:23)
- **Hear/Listen** - (Matthew 11:15; Mark 4:9) Most people think that you can only hear/listen with your ears. There is more to listening than hearing words. Learn to listen with your ears, your eyes, your spirit and conscience.

- o You may ask, how do you hear with your eyes? People will sometimes say one thing verbally with their mouths, but their expressions and mannerisms tell a different story. Be observant and listen with your ears and with your eyes. There are numerous references in the Bible to the "countenance" – physical appearance or expression -- change that occurred in people during various situations. (Genesis 4:5-6; 31:2-5; Judges 13:6; 1 Samuel 16:7; Nehemiah 2:2; Psalm 42:11; Proverbs 15:13; Matthew 28:3; Revelation 1:16).
- o Be swift to hear, slow to speak, slow to wrath (James 1:19-20). Listen carefully before you speak. Don't ignore your conscience (John 8:9; Acts 23:1; 24:16; Romans 2:15; 9:1; 2 Corinthians 4:1-6).

- **Hold on to the promise; don't dwell on the past.**
(Philippians 3:13-14) Paul said that he pressed toward the mark/goal for the prize of the high calling of God in Christ. He knew a prize was waiting for him in heaven, so that is what he focused on. Hold on to the promise and God's word. **Let go of disappointments, bitterness, strife, self-pity, and anger** (Ephesians 4:30-32). Abraham received the promise years before Isaac was born. Be patient and learn to wait on God to fulfill His promises.
  - o Hold on; don't give up. Hurts heal with time and with God's help. Often, the physical hurts heal quicker than the mental and emotional hurts. You may not forget the situation that

caused the hurt, but over time and with God's help, the emotions associated with the situation can't hold you captive, **unless you let it**.

- **Remind yourself of God's goodness, of what He has done, and of what He can do**. At one of the churches I attended, we sang a verse that said: "I've got a little bitty problem, but a great big God!" God is bigger and more powerful than any problem you will ever have. **Study Psalm 103 and tell your soul to bless the Lord! Don't forget what He has done** (Proverbs 3:1-10).
  - o **Stop hiding, stop running away from God and run to God**. You really can't hide; he sees you, he knows what you have done and what you haven't done. He wants you to confess your sins. Read Genesis chapter three. After Adam and Eve sinned and they heard the voice of God, they hid. God called to Adam and asked where he was. Adam replied, "I heard thy voice in the garden and **I was afraid**, because I was naked, and **I hid** myself." Later in the conversation, we can see where blaming others - a.k.a. passing the buck - began. Adam told God that it was the woman that God gave him that led to him eating, so he blamed Eve for giving him the fruit, and Eve blamed the serpent for misleading or deceiving her. The serpent had no one to blame but himself, but he didn't accept any blame. Punishments were given to each of them, but God also gave hope for redemption for Adam and Eve and their offspring

(verse 15 refers to the seed of the woman which will bruise the head of the serpent. Jesus is that seed.) God showed grace by making Adam and Eve clothing before sending them from the garden. Too often, we try to hide our sin because of fear. This is the wrong thing to do. God sees you, even when others don't. **What's done in the dark will come to the light**. Your sin will find you out. (Numbers 32:23)

- o **Don't focus on your problems, but rather, keep your eyes on Jesus**. Peter was able to walk on water as long as he kept his eyes on Jesus. However, when he took his eyes off Jesus and focused on the boisterous/violent winds, he became afraid and began to sink. Circumstances can cause you to become distracted. Then, you focus on the problem. When this happens, ask Jesus for help. I find it interesting that the wind ceased when they came into the ship (Matthew 14:14-32).

- **Take responsibility for your actions**. Confess your faults (James 5:16); speak the truth in love (Ephesians 4:15). Confess your sin. If we confess our sins, he is faithful and just to forgive us our sins, and to cleanse us from all unrighteousness. (1 John 1:9)

- **Take the high road and the narrow path**. You don't have to trample over others or sink to their level to get ahead. Do things God's way and follow his path, even when it's not convenient, not popular, or when it goes against the world's standards (Matthew 7:14).

- **Let God be God, and you be you**. There are things in this life that only God can handle. Stay in God's peace (Philippians 4: 6-7). All your worrying won't change anything. I like this saying that has been attributed to Erma Bombeck: "Worry is just like a rocking chair; it gives you something to do, but it never gets you anywhere." Worrying changes nothing.
  - o Vengeance belongs to God....not to you (Romans 12:19). He even tells us in Proverbs 24:17-18 and verse 29 that we should not rejoice over our enemies' calamities or misfortunes.
  - o You weren't designed to carry worry (Matthew 6:25-34). Jesus said, *"Come unto me all ye that labour and are heaven laden, and I will give you rest. Take my yoke upon you and learn of me; for I am meek and lowly in heart: and ye shall find rest unto your souls."* (Matthew 11:28-29). Cast your cares upon him because He cares for you (1 Peter 5:7).

- **Stop pretending that you've always been saved and never made mistakes**. For all have sinned...Romans 3:23). We've all messed up in life...numerous times, so don't be surprised when others fail.

- **Do what Jesus says to do.** Example: At the marriage feast, Mary said these words to the servants: "Whatsoever he saith unto you, do it." (John 2:5). The servants obeyed Jesus, and a miracle happened. Focus on Jesus and be like him…he is our example. Do what he says.

- o   He knew his mission was to do the Father's will and not his own; to lose nothing the Father had given him; and to give everlasting life to those who believe in him (John 6:38-40).
- o   Jesus said that only those who do the Father's will would enter the kingdom of heaven (Matthew 7:21).
- o   Be a doer of the word and not just a hearer. If you just hear and don't do, you deceive yourself. (James 1:22-27)

- **Study the Word, read the Word, and do the good works he has prepared for you to do.** Live the Word and seek God to find out your purpose and calling (2 Timothy 2:15; 3:16-17; Ephesians 2:10).

   - o   **Seek knowledge.** Sometimes it's the things we don't know that cause us problems. An even deeper thought is: it is what we don't know that we don't know that also causes us problems. The prophet Hosea said that God's people were destroyed because they lacked knowledge and because they had rejected knowledge (Hosea 4:6). How many times have we been hurt, lost things of value, not received a blessing, etc., because we didn't have the wisdom and knowledge we needed? People have even committed crimes because they were ignorant of the laws that were in place.

- **Be open to hear wisdom and seek wisdom and understanding** (Proverbs 4:5-7; 16:16). Remember, you can learn something from almost any one…even those you might think are the least among you. Ask God for wisdom (James 1:5-8).

- o **Don't be ashamed of the gospel of Christ** for it is the power of God unto salvation to everyone that believes (Romans 1:16-17).
- o **Confess Jesus before men and He will confess you before His Father** (Matthew 10:32-33 & Luke 12:8-10).

- **Prepare in advance for what you are expecting**; i.e., baby, spouse, house, job, etc.
  - o Proverbs 30:25 gives examples of how ants are little and not strong. Ants are very wise because they prepare their food in the summer in anticipation of it not being available when winter comes. We can learn how to plan and prepare from ants. They don't let their size keep them from accomplishing their goals.

- **Humble yourself** – be humble. Don't be high minded nor lifted up (Romans 11:17-20; 1 Timothy 6:17-19; 2 Timothy 3:1-17). God resists the proud but gives grace to the humble (James 4:6-10 & 1 Peter 5:5). Pride comes before destruction (Proverbs 18:12). It's all about His grace and His mercy. He has gifted it to us, we can't earn it; we don't deserve it (Romans 5:15; 11:6; Ephesians 2:5-8; 3:7). Don't think that you are better than people who are not yet where you are on this journey. If we didn't have God's grace, we could be where they are now or even worse (1 Corinthians 15:10).

- Once you are saved/born again, and you start learning the truth, it can be so easy to think that you have arrived and are better than those who don't believe like you do. Some of this is pride, some is ignorance, and some is deception. Don't forget that you were once lost, too, and that we've all sinned and fallen short of the glory of God!!!
- **What does it mean to be humble?** It is defined in various ways, but one definition is to be meek and submissive to the divine will. Jesus humbled himself and became obedient to death – even the death of the cross (Philippians 2:8). He told us to humble ourselves as children (Matthew 18:4; 23:12). Other scriptures on humility are: Proverbs 22:4; Luke 18:17; John 13:6-14; Philippians 2:5-9; Colossians 2:18.

- **Focus on what you have and on what you can do instead of dwelling on what you don't have or what you can't do.** Sometimes we get so focused on what we can't have or what we can't do, that we lose sight of all the things we have. I've been guilty of this, especially when trying to lose weight. I initially focus on not being able to eat all my favorite foods to the degree I want to and lose sight of all the wonderful foods that are available for me to eat. Love yourself and get your focus right.
  - **Genesis 2:8-9** tells us that God planted a garden and put Adam in it. He also made every tree grow that is pleasant to

the sight and good for food. He also made the tree of life and the tree of the knowledge of good and evil.

- o **In Genesis 2:16-17** Adam was told that he could eat freely of every tree of the garden except the tree of the knowledge of good and evil.
- o **Genesis 3:1-6** - The serpent focused Eve's attention on the one thing she was forbidden to eat, rather than on the unlimited number of trees she could eat from.

Chapter 10: Love Your Neighbor As Yourself

- **Treat people right -** Do unto others as you would have them do unto you. (Matthew 7:12 and Luke 6:31). See also 1 Corinthians 13.

    o Honor/obey your parents and treat your children right. (Exodus 20:12; Deuteronomy 5:16; Ephesians 6:1-4)

    o If you don't want people to steal from you, then don't steal. If you had your own business and you were paying someone to work for you, you'd expect a full day's work for a full day's pay; do the same when you work for someone else.

    o If you want someone to keep things in confidence and not gossip or talk behind your back, then you keep confidence and don't gossip or talk behind the back of others.

    o If you want others to respect you, your property, your children, and your marriage, then, you do the same.

    o Do you want someone to laugh at you when you are hurting, embarrassed, or make a mistake? Then treat others the same way you want to be treated.

    o If you want someone to be faithful to you, then be faithful. You can only control your actions. You can't control the actions of others. You aren't even responsible for the actions of others. We must each give account to God for the things we do (Romans 14:12 & 2 Corinthians 5:10). Just because you do what's right doesn't mean that others will do the same. Remember: vengeance belongs to God (Romans 12:19-21).

o If you want God to forgive you, then you must forgive others. Holding grudges and unforgiveness hurts you. It does not hurt the other person. The other people have probably already moved on, while you're still stuck holding on to the offense and you are miserable. There is a quote by Marianne Williamson that says: "Unforgiveness is like drinking poison yourself and waiting for the other person to die." The only person you are hurting is yourself. **Release yourself. Let it go!** Love, bless, and pray for your enemies and those who have persecuted you or despitefully used you (Matthew 5:44 and Luke 6:28). **Ask God to help you forgive.** It's hard to do this without His help. **It is a choice that only you can make.**

o If you want others to respect you and listen to your opinions, then be willing to listen to the opinion of others, even if you disagree with them. Disagree civilly – you won't agree with everything you hear. That's ok, but you don't have to be mean and rude and violent about it. A soft answer turns away wrath. (Proverbs 15:1)

o If you are a guest in someone's home, then be a good guest. Don't treat their home the way you would treat a hotel. You aren't paying to stay there, so contribute: help with dishes, meals, clean the room you're in, respect the rules your host has for his/her home. Don't overstay your welcome. "Withdraw thy foot from thy neighbour's house, lest he be weary of thee and so hate thee." (Proverbs 25:17)

o   Be a good host/hostess. If you invite someone to your home, prepare for their arrival. Make them feel welcome. If you have standards and rules for your home, let them know what they are. It's better to share this up front than to get in strife because they broke a rule of yours that you didn't tell them about.

o   Help other people when you can.

- **Your children are a part of you, and if they are born again, they are also your brothers and sisters in Christ**

- They are watching you, hearing you, and learning from your examples. **Teach your children:**

o   **To have fun.** Spend time with your children. Don't let the phones, tablets, TV, games and technology take over your responsibility. Play games with them. Let your house be the house they want to spend time in. Make up your own games and traditions. My children and I made up the "sentence" game, license plate game and math game while we were in the car together. It made time pass by faster, kept everyone listening and engaged; and it was fun.

o   **To fight laziness and slothfulness** (Proverbs 18:9; 26:13-16; Romans 12:10-11; Hebrews 6:11-12). Habits - good or bad - that we pick up as children, often carry on into adulthood — exhibit good habits to them.

- ○ **To take good advice and receive correction** (Proverbs 12:15; 13:10-18). Wise children listen to their parents. (Proverbs 13:1)

- ○ **Discipline and self-control**. Discipline is defined as the practice of training people to obey rules or a code of behavior, using punishment to correct disobedience. All Bible references here will be from the Message Bible: Proverbs 13:24: "A refusal to correct is a refusal to love; love your children by disciplining them." "Kids who lash out against their parents are an embarrassment and disgrace." (Proverbs 19:26) Discipline your children while you still have the chance; spoiling them and indulging them can destroy them (Proverbs 19:18). "Point your kids in the right direction –when they're old, they won't be lost." (Proverbs 22:6)

  - ▪ **God disciplines/corrects/chastens His children** (Proverbs 3:11-12; Hebrews 12:6-13)

  - ▪ **Discipline doesn't mean to beat, misuse, mistreat, disfigure, belittle, kill, or break your children physically, mentally, spiritually,** or **emotionally.**

  - ▪ **Self-control or temperance** is one of the fruits of the Spirit. The power to control our actions and thoughts rests with us.

- Responsibility – start when they are young. Give them chores and responsibilities that are age-appropriate; i.e., folding face towels, picking up toys, washing dishes, making up their beds, vacuuming, etc. Chores teach them responsibility. Show them what to do and how to do it.
- To respect: parents, authority, themselves, others and most importantly, God.
- How to read, study, and gain understanding. Also, teach them when and how to ask questions. Help them with homework, but also help them study the Bible and memorize scripture. Sometimes you need to personalize the Word of God. When going through specific trials, I spent time confessing the promises in Psalm 34, 37, and 91.
- Dependability – My dad used to say, "Let your word be your bond." People should be able to count on you to do what you committed to doing, as long as it's not illegal or immoral or unethical.
- Perseverance – Endure until the end (Matthew 10:22; 24:6-13; Mark 13:13). Run your race with patience looking to Jesus and don't faint in your minds (Hebrews 12:1-3). Remind them to be careful with their thoughts. Your thoughts and what you dwell on can cause you to give up or do things you may regret later.
- Delayed gratification. Show them how to be patient and how to wait.

- We don't always get what we want when we want it.
- Wait on God. He doesn't always move when we want Him to move. He is not a genie. HE IS GOD.
- Save for items you want rather than charging them on a credit card. If you use a credit card, practice paying off your cards before you incur interest. Show them how to shop for bargains and to wait for items to go on sale.
- Start investing early.
- Wait for the right relationships, friends, and spouse.

o **Common Sense.** Sometimes I wonder what ever happened to people using common sense. Then, I realize that my problem is that I am assuming that someone has taught them certain things about life. In some cases, people haven't been taught. I encourage you to teach your kids - the ordinary things as well as the things they need to know to prosper in life. Don't just tell them to do something and expect them to do it right if you haven't taught them how to do it. Show them how to clean, do laundry, make up the bed, cook, set up and handle a budget, shop, solve problems, talk calmly to others, self-defense, etc.

o **Communication** – how to write, listen and talk; when to talk, when to be quiet, when to share and the types of things to share as well as the things they should keep as private.

- **How to Pray** – let them hear you pray so they can learn from you. Let them hear you bless your food, pray for them, for others, situations in life, etc. Part of praying involves forgiving others, letting go of offenses, and not seeking vengeance. Forgiveness is a choice that needs to be made daily. Do not give others control of your life by dwelling on an offense. Give it to God.

- **To be grateful and to give thanks.** Too often, I see children who expect to receive everything they ask for, and then when they get it, they don't appreciate it. We should give thanks for what we have. I'm more apt to give more to a grateful person than to someone who is a complainer that doesn't value what they've been given, and who always wants more. David wrote concerning God, "Enter into his gates with thanksgiving, and into his courts with praise: be thankful unto him, and bless his name." (Psalms 100:4). God wants us to be thankful.

  Find things to be thankful for, even when things aren't going the way you want them to. We are blessed. There are many people who would love to have just a portion of what we take for granted every day. Find joy in the simple things in life.

- **To serve with honor, humility, honesty, and excellence;** whether working in food service, helping out at home, taking care of someone, or working on a job.

- To be content. (Philippians 4:11; 1 Timothy 4:6-12; Hebrews 13:5) These scriptures speak about being content; not in the sense of giving up, but of not coveting what others have and trusting God to provide for our needs.

- **Bless your children with words, actions, and examples** - Let them know that they are children of possibility and children of promise. Speak words of encouragement to them. Do not belittle your children. Do not provoke them. (Ephesians 6:4)
  - I was intentional about not calling my children "bad" when they did terrible things. Instead, I said they were busy or not behaving right. I never wanted the word "bad" to be associated with who they were and are.
  - Listen to your children.
  - Protect your children. Don't expose your kids to everyone you know or everyone you date. Don't leave them alone with people who could compromise their safety, hurt them, expose them to things like drugs, porn, weapons, etc. Know what your children are watching on television and online. Know what they are reading, who they are talking to, texting, etc. Periodically check your minor children's phones, computer, search history, etc. Know their friends and who will be in the homes of friends if they go to sleepovers.

- **Share your testimony** - Talk about God's goodness. Don't be ashamed of Him. My family and I grew up poor, in a very rural area in Mississippi. I wore hand me down clothes. Neither of my parents finished high school. However, they raised 9 children. Seven of us went to college and earned bachelor and master's degrees. One received an associate degree, and only one never went to college.

I was divorced at an early age. At the time of my separation, my children were 11 months, 23 months, 3 years old, and 5-year-old twins. With initially very little and then later no child support, God opened doors for me and provided for my family and me. We overcame by the blood of the lamb and the word of our testimony (Revelation 12:11). His grace sustained us. His word encouraged us. One morning while praying with friends, a specific word that I was given to stand on was Psalm 115:14. The verse states: "The Lord shall increase you more and more, you and your children." I held on to that promise, even when it seemed like nothing good was happening in my life. God has been faithful and continues to fulfill that promise.

- **Give:**
    - **And it will be given to you**.... (Luke 6:38)
    - **Purposefully & cheerfully.** God loves a cheerful giver. (2 Corinthians 9:7)
    - **Obediently and prove God** (Malachi 3:10-12)
    - **To the poor and be blessed** (Proverbs 19:17; 22:9-16; & 28:27; 29:7)

Jot down your key learnings from Part III:

_____

_____

_____

_____

_____

My questions from Part III:

_____

_____

_____

_____

_____

_____

_____

_____

_____

_____

_____

_____

_____

_____

_____

PART IV: GG's LIFE NUGGETS

Chapter 11: GG's Life Nuggets

This chapter is composed of things I've learned over the years and consider them to be valuable advice and nuggets of wisdom for you to think about.

- **Choose wisely** - We were created with "free will" and the ability to choose. Your choices lead to actions, and your actions have consequences. Although you can make choices, you don't always control the consequences of your actions. The consequences may be decided by someone else. What you do affects you as well as other people. Some consequences are good, some are bad. Some have short-term effects, some have long term effects, and some have lifelong and generational effects. You've probably heard the saying, "what goes around comes around." Well, the biblical text for this is: "Be not deceived; God is not mocked: for whatsoever a man soweth, that shall he also reap." (Galatians 6:7)
  - **Make wise choices in your friends, spouse, jobs, etc.** Surround yourself with the right people: people you can learn from, people you can trust, people who will tell you what you need to know and not just what you want to hear, people who will encourage you to do right and will lift you up and not put you down. Choose friends wisely. Remember, over time, you tend to pick up some of their habits and ways of thinking.

- Choose wisely when you have an opportunity to hire; regardless of if you're hiring a babysitter or a CEO. The decision that individual makes will have consequences for you and other people.
- Choose whom you will serve. (Joshua 24:15). I've heard people say, "no one can tell me what to do." Then later when they are in jail, someone tells them when to wake up, when to sleep, when they can shower, where they can go, who they can talk to, when they can use the bathroom, etc.
  - We either serve God, or we serve the devil. No man can serve two masters. (Matthew 6:24; Luke 16:13). We can make the decision each day whom we will serve.
- Choose names and nicknames for your children that are positive, that encourage them and that build them up. Don't say things like, "you're good for nothing, you'll never amount to anything, you're going to end up in jail, you're crazy, you're stupid, etc." If you do this, then don't be surprised when what you say becomes a reality because your child has internalized what they've heard from you. As Rachel was dying, she named her newborn son Ben-oni, meaning son of my sorrow. Jacob renamed him Benjamin or son of my right hand or son of the south so that the child wouldn't be reminded of the sorrow of his mother's death every time he heard his name (Genesis 35:18).

- **Use your imagination for good, to see possibilities, and to solve problems.** (2 Corinthians 10:5) We are to cast down imaginations of things that exalt themselves against the knowledge of Christ and to capture our thoughts to the obedience of Christ. There are things we can think about that are good (Philippians 4:8). When dealing with problems, ask God for help.
  - Think outside the box.
  - Make others aware of problems, but also bring solutions to those problems.
  - There is great value in solving problems. Most inventions come as a result of solving a problem or meeting a need. <u>You can change your life with just one unique idea, properly executed, that is of value to others.</u>

- **Don't let your past define your future.** Unfortunately, we can't change our history. We can regret it, apologize for it, embrace it, learn from it, etc. The apostle Paul said that one thing he did was "forgetting those things which are behind and reaching forth unto those things which are before. I press toward the mark for the prize of the high calling of God in Christ Jesus." (Philippians 3:13-14). Sometimes the past isn't easy to forget or let go of, which is why we need a savior. "Therefore if any man be in Christ, he is a new creature: old things are passed away; behold, all things are become new." (2 Corinthians 5:17). This applies to men, women, boys, and girls. It's why Jesus said we must be born again.

Do you remember your past? Yes. Will other people remember your past? Yes, they will. However, God has this amazing ability to forget. When he declares you not guilty, He sees what Jesus did when he died for our sins, instead of seeing what we did. (See: Psalm 103:12; Jeremiah 31:34; and Hebrews 8:8-13)

- **Pursue excellence**: God sets the standards for excellence. So do your best: Use the gifts and talents you have. We don't all have the same talents, but we can all use our talents. **So, pursue excellence in:**
  - work (Work as unto God – Colossians 3:23-25)
  - chores
  - school
  - serving God
  - your home
  - relationships

- **Lift up your head, your eyes and your posture.** Carry yourself in the right way. If you can, stand erect—not hunched over. Looking down can reflect low self-esteem and low self-worth. Make good eye contact when talking to others – but don't "stare them down."

- **Endure pruning** – let God rub off your rough edges. He may use people and circumstances to help do this. It may not be comfortable, but it will be designed to make you stronger. God chastens those He loves (Hebrews 12:5-11).

- **Control your tongue and your temper**. Speak words of encouragement. Speak the truth in love. Use your tongue to build up and not tear down. Sometimes it's not just what you say, but how you say it (Proverbs 15:1-4). Choose your words wisely. Know when to be silent. The tongue can be poisonous (James 3:8-10).

- **Handle money wisely – give, save, invest, eliminate debt, look for bargains.**
  - Pay your bills. When you borrow money or buy on credit, you give your word that you will pay it back. Do the right thing. Would you want someone to borrow from you and then not pay you back?
  - Save money regularly. Read the story of Oseola McCarty, a black woman in Mississippi with a sixth-grade education who donated $150,000 to the University of Mississippi so that black students could get an education. Her only job had been doing laundry for others; i.e., washing and ironing clothes. She was a diligent saver. God takes pleasure in the prosperity of his people (Psalm 35:27)
  - Give - see the earlier section on giving on page 90.
  - Invest to increase value (Matthew 25:24-30). Also, invest in people.
  - Eliminate debt when possible. – owe no man anything but to love one another (Romans 13:8). The borrower is a servant to the lender (Proverbs 22:7). Don't become a slave to debt.

- **Let go of the works of the flesh and put on the fruit of the spirit.** Study Galatians 5:19-26.
    - ○ **Be transformed by the renewing of your mind** (Romans 12:1-2). Think about the process of going from an ugly caterpillar to a beautiful butterfly. Without Christ, we are unclean, and our righteousness is as filthy rags (Isaiah 64:6)
    - ○ **"Let all bitterness and indignation and wrath (passion, rage, bad temper) and resentment (anger, animosity) and quarreling (brawling, clamor, contention) and slander (evil-speaking, abusive or blasphemous language) be banished from you, with all malice (spite, ill will, or baseness of any kind).** And become useful and helpful and kind to one another, tenderhearted (compassionate, understanding, loving-hearted), forgiving one another (readily and freely), as God in Christ forgave you." (Ephesians 4:31-32 Amplified Bible)
- **Live in the present:** You can't change the past. You can repent of it, learn from it, and regret it, but you can't change it. You can dream about tomorrow and plan for it, but tomorrow is not promised to you. We live in the present. Make the most of it! (Matthew 6:34; Proverbs 27:1; James 4:13-17)
- **Live your own life; don't try to live the life of others.** Each of us has our own skills, abilities, needs, wants, and purpose. Find out what yours are. Don't get caught up in trying to be like everyone else. God has a plan for you. Find out what God's plan is

for you and live it. Don't covet anything that belongs to someone else (Exodus 20:17).

- **Defrost** – unfreeze from the past. When I was young, we played the game, freeze and defrost. Music would play, and the leader would randomly tell us to "freeze." At that moment we were supposed to stop what we were doing and remain in that position/condition until we were told to "defrost," and then we could resume playing the game. Has something happened in your life that has caused you to "freeze" and you haven't been able to move forward? Are you reliving a hurt that happened a long time ago and everyone has moved on except you? It's time to "DEFROST!" Confess the issue or circumstance to God. Tell Him how you feel. Release it to Him and ask Him to heal you. Each time the thought or feeling of anger comes, remember that it's under the blood of Jesus. Refuse to take it back. Pray for those that despitefully use you (Matthew 5:44-48 & Luke 6:28-36). **As long as you are still alive, you have the ability and opportunity to change things.**

- **Don't let pride get in the way of you being reconciled to God**. You can't "out sin" God's grace…. He forgives all manner of sin and blasphemy, except blasphemy against the Holy Ghost. (Matthew 12:31)

- **Don't live in the land of "pity parties" and excuses**. "Excuses are just like a behind, everybody's got one." There are lots of examples of people who overcame adversity, poverty, sickness. Research: Wilma Rudolph, Venus and Serena Williams, Mae Lemke, your great grandparents & me. Take the initiative and do what you can do. Be thankful for what you have. Take one step at a time. See setbacks as opportunities to build muscles and as potential "setups" to overcome adversity. **Pity party** land is not a good place to camp out in or to make a home. There are times when we all become discouraged. Things don't always go the way we want them to go. It's easy to start thinking, "poor me, nothing ever goes right for me. Things are never going to change or get better. I wish I was like......." These tips may help you escape the land of pity parties.

- o **Stop the negative self-talk!** Be realistic. If you need professional help, get it. Put on some happy or praise music. Be thankful for what you have. Make a list of things you are thankful for. I'm sure if you look long enough you could find someone who wishes they had what you have. I've worked with and seen people who were blind – totally and legally—people with MS, diabetes, partially paralyzed, one or more limbs missing, etc. Their disabilities didn't preclude them from working, smiling, and enjoying life.

- o **Look beyond your current circumstances.** Where you are now is a fact. But facts represent a single point in time. Facts are subject to change. Jesus endured the cross for the joy that was set before him. He knew the reality of where he was, was subject to change.

  I saw the twins in a dream before they were born. In the dream, they were about two (2) years old. The twins were born two (2) months premature, and each weighed two pounds thirteen ounces (2 lbs. 13 oz). Because of the dream God had given me, I knew they were going to be alright. The premature birth wasn't the end of their story. It became a testimony!

- o **Know you gain strength through resistance**; i.e., weightlifting, trials, etc. We all have the same number of muscles. Our strength depends on how we develop them. The more resistance you use in weight training, the stronger your muscles will become. There is danger in comfort and inaction. If you stop using your muscles, they will atrophy and will not retain their strength. Use what you have been given. Don't lose it. Learn from and gain strength from your struggles. (James 1:1-4)

- o **Prepare for opportunities long before they appear.** Be diligent. David prepared for war while he was a shepherd and protecting his sheep from lions, wolves, and bears. Joseph prepared for leadership while a slave and in prison. Mothers prepare for babies while they are pregnant. Don't wait for a particular condition to happen before you prepare. By then, it may be too late.

- o **Be faithful in the small things, in the ordinary and mundane things as well as the large things.** If you aren't faithful in little things, you may never get an opportunity to do greater things. Do your work without complaining. Watch

/adjust your attitude. You just might be in training and being prepared to do something greater. (Moses spent 40 years in the desert as a shepherd. David was a shepherd before he became king. Joseph was a slave and a prisoner before he became second in charge of Egypt.) Sometimes we see people's successes, but never see the weeks, months, and years of struggles and preparation it took them to become successful.

- **Show initiative:** Initiative is defined as the ability to assess and initiate things independently; the power or opportunity to act or take charge before others do so, or a fresh approach to something. In other words, if you see something that needs to be done and you can do it, then, do it. Make sure it's legal and moral.

    o **Be diligent and use your gifts.** "Observe people who are good at their work—skilled workers are always in demand and admired; they don't take a backseat to anyone." (Proverbs 22:29 Message Bible). God's gifts and calling are without repentance. (Romans 11:27-32).

    o **Do your best.** Don't live in the land of mediocrity by just doing enough to get by. Remember your best may not be someone else's best. You are only accountable to God for using the "talents" He has given to you.

- **Not everything that feels good, looks good or tastes good is good for you.** "There is a way which seemeth right unto a man, but the end thereof are the ways of death." (Proverbs 14:12;

& 16:25). "Every way of a man is right in his own eyes: but the Lord pondereth the hearts" (Proverbs 21:2). People have become addicted and led into bondage because of things that look, feel, and taste good. God knows what's best for you; so if He says, "no" or "no not now", trust that He has your best interest at heart. He sees beyond what we see.

- **Run your own race**. There is only one you. Focus on what you are designed to do. Stop worrying about what others have and what they are doing. You are unique. You are you for a purpose. Finish your race, and you will receive a crown. There is an interesting story in John 21:1-22 when Jesus appeared after his resurrection. He talked to Peter and told Peter how he would die (vs. 18-19). Peter then asked Jesus, "and what shall this man do?" (vs. 21). Jesus answered and said, *"If I will that he tarry till I come, what is that to thee? Follow thou me."* In other words, do what I tell you to do and don't worry about what I have for the other disciple to do. Peter's job was to follow Jesus.

- **Beware that in your desire to be free from rules, discipline and to be independent from God, you may unknowingly become a slave to something else.**

- **Your attitude matters.** Watch your attitude and adjust it when needed. Sometimes it's not what you say but how you say it. People can hear your attitude by how you speak – tone, inflections, word choice, etc., but they can also see your attitude by how you look, react, and in what you do and don't do. Be a thermostat, not a thermometer. Don't just react to what goes on around you. Instead, set the tone and influence your environment.

- o When your attitude changes, your countenance/appearance/expressions may also change.
- o Attitude determines your altitude. Zig Ziglar said, "It is your attitude, more than your aptitude that will determine your altitude." You can be very knowledgeable and do excellent work; but if you can't get along with people, have a negative attitude, or have low self-esteem, you may not progress. You can have a beautiful face and body, but also have a nasty attitude, and you will turn people away. People like to work with and for people with a good attitude. It can even affect team sports. One member of a team with a bad attitude can change how well or how poorly the team performs.

- **Protect the things that are important to you.** It's so easy for us to get our priorities out of order. Align your actions with what you say are your priorities:
  - o **People & relationships.** Once while I was in a leadership class, there was a scenario involving a group of people. The question posed to each group was, "How close to the edge of the cliff are you willing to take your family to win the competition?" Lots of answers came back, including someone who said, "all the way to the edge." The real

answer is: if you value them, you won't take them towards danger, but you will always keep them away from it.

- o **Property** – lock your doors and windows (this includes your home, your vehicles, etc.) When you're pumping gas, lock your car doors. Keep your purse out of sight and on the floor near you.
- o **Dreams & ideas** - don't let people steal them, cheat you out of them, or discourage you from pursuing them. Seek God about which dreams to pursue.
- o **Value true friends** (Proverbs 17:17; 18:24). True friends are rare.
- o **Value your family – parents, siblings, children, spouse, etc.** Treat them the way you want to be treated. Build them up and don't tear them down. Speak words of encouragement. Spend quality time with them. Show them in little and big ways that they are important to you. Let them know they are more important than work and your friends.
- o **YOU** – you are worth fighting for. Get checkups, eat right, and get appropriate rest. You only get one body. If you don't fight for yourself, who will? If you are not willing to invest in yourself, why should someone else invest in you?

- **Don't tell others about things you have that could lead to them coveting** it or stealing it or hurting you to get it. "Gossips can't keep secrets, so never confide in blabbermouths" (Proverbs 20:19 Message Bible).

- **Park near or under a light when you park at night. Be safe and observe your surroundings.**

- **Drive carefully and defensively.** Just because you have the right of way doesn't mean you should proceed. Move when it's safe to move.

- **Count your change and review your order before you leave a place.** Do it preferably in the presence of the person who you purchased from. People can make mistakes and most are willing to fix them. It's easier for them to recognize the issue if you show the person their mistake when it happens and before you walk away.

- **If you find yourself in a hole, stop digging**! Ask for help. Ask for instructions and help on how to do something when you need it. Don't be ashamed to ask for forgiveness.

- **Ask the right questions.** If you don't ask the right question, you may not get the answers you need. Ask open-ended questions and not just questions requiring a "yes" or "no" answer. When you've exhausted all you know to ask, think about asking, "what question haven't I asked that would help me better assess the situation or respond to the issue?"

- **When people show you who they are, believe them!** If they show you through their actions that they are a liar, cheater, thief, or violent, then they are showing you their heart. Most people focus on just the big things and overlook some of the smaller things. Solomon said the little foxes spoil the vines. (Song of Solomon

2:15). A decimal in the wrong place changes a dollar amount. For example, if you have the numbers 1000 and tell someone to put a decimal anywhere in that group of numbers, then that little decimal matters. Place it before the 1 and the number becomes .1000; place it after the last 0 and the number is 1000. If this represents dollars, would you rather have ten cents or a thousand dollars? Little things also matter and can be hints of things to come.

- **Speak up – tell somebody if someone hurts you or threatens you**; if they don't believe you, tell someone else.

- **Don't major on the minors** – sometimes we focus on style, looks, clothes, color, etc. Even when raising our children, we sometimes focus on the minor things. I've been guilty of this. Pick your fights...not everything should lead to an argument or a debate. Think about this: if the things you are complaining about were the last words you had an opportunity to speak to a loved one, **is it worth it**?

- **Dress appropriately.** Dress for the job you want. Dress for the occasion. Don't over or under dress. You don't have to go into debt to impress. Find bargains and sales. Shop at thrift and consignment stores. Some people donate nice clothing to Goodwill & Salvation Army stores or have nice things at garage sales. Watch the paper for sales and use coupons. Be neat and clean. Take care of what you have.

- **Plan for maintenance of your vehicles, your house, yourself.**

- ○ Buy insurance (auto, home, renters, life, health, flood)
- ○ Nothing lasts forever. Things will need to be repaired or replaced, so save in advance for these things.
- ○ Get annual checkups, groom properly, rest, relax, fix yourself up, exercise, etc.

- **Take a self-defense class.**

- **Don't carry a lot of cash; and if you do, don't let people see it.**

- **Learn from your mistakes.** Don't keep making the same mistake over and over again.

- **Don't say everything you think.** You may regret it later.

- **Seek peace** (Psalm 34:14; Matthew 5:9; Romans 12:18-21) rather than confrontation.

- **Stay away from profanity and corrupt communication.** (Psalm 34:13; Proverbs 13:3 & Ephesians 4:29-30)

- **Trust God and obey Him out of love, not out of fear.** Jesus said, "If you love me, keep my commandments." (John 14:15).

- **Ask God for what you need, seek Him and knock for it.** Keep asking. (Matthew 7:7-11). If you need help from people, ask for it. Don't get in the habit of relying on the support from people long term. Don't let the help become a crutch. Remember, God is your source. Ask God for wisdom (James 1:5)

- **Trust but verify** - while a source of information might be considered reliable, you should perform additional research to confirm that the information is accurate, or trustworthy; especially when you have others help you with your finances. Many people have trusted financial advisors, employees, and even some friends and family members with their money only to find out later that it has been stolen, misused, or lost.

- **Avoid co-signing for others.** (Proverbs 17:18; 22:26-27) I learned this lesson the hard way and co-signed to help a relative. Needless to say, they defaulted, and I ended up having to pay the balance. I will not co-sign again for anyone.

- **Dance** – it's good exercise (David danced). It's fun. Let everything be done decently and in order. Dancing can be a way to stay fit for people of all ages, shapes and sizes. It has a wide range of physical and mental benefits, including:
  - improved conditioning for your heart and lungs, better aerobic fitness, which leads to improved muscle tone and strength
  - weight management, increased physical confidence, greater self-confidence and self-esteem, which could help with social skills
  - stronger bones and reduced risk of some diseases, better coordination, agility, balance and flexibility
  - improved mental functioning

- **Laugh when it's appropriate**– a merry heart doeth good like a medicine (Proverbs 15:13; 17:22). Even God laughs (Psalm 2:4; 37:12-13). Laughter isn't appropriate when it hurts others. Research says that laughter helps with the following things:
  - relaxation, boosting the immune system, reducing stress, improving circulation, decreases the secretion of epinephrine and cortisol, improves your mood, may help prevent heart disease, helps shifts your perspective so that you can see more possibilities, and fosters emotional connections with others.
  - The joy of the Lord is your strength (Nehemiah 8:10).
- **Count the cost before you start a project or course of action and make sure you have the funds, knowledge, skills, etc., to complete it** (Luke 14:28-33).
- **Jesus should take priority in our lives.** John the Baptist said that Jesus must increase, but he must decrease (John 3:30). That's good advice.
- **Know your seasons:** There is a season for everything (Ecclesiastes 3). There are seasons you encounter in life that are somewhat similar to the seasons in the weather.
  - Spring – things are planted, and sometimes things begin to sprout and blossom (this may resemble the early stages in life or when your career is just starting to take off.)

- Summer – Plants are in full bloom. People are active and spend time outside. The sun shines longer than other times of the year. There will be seasons in life where you feel everything is going well and you are enjoying life. You have health and strength and a body you like. Your thought processes are quick, and you have plenty of friends. Your career has taken off, and you're doing well.

- Fall – leaves begin to fall; colors begin to change. At some point in life, things will start to change. You may not be as strong or as healthy. Your body begins to change. Your career may plateau, life changes around you.

- Winter – plants appear dead, it may be cold, windy, snowy and icy. Things may seem unbearable. Cold and flu season may be prevalent. The sun shines less because the days are shorter and nighttime is longer. In the winter of life, sickness, disease and injury may be more frequent. You may lose more friends and loved ones. Life slows down. It appears death may be near. But remember: spring is coming!

Jot down your key learnings from Part IV:

_____

_____

_____

_____

_____

_____

_____

_____

_____

_____

_____

_____

_____

_____

_____

_____

_____

_____

_____

_____

_____

_____

_____

My questions from Part IV:

_____

_____

_____

_____

_____

_____

_____

_____

_____

_____

_____

_____

_____

PART V: Blessings

Family Blessing

I decree this blessing upon my family:

That you will be blessed to know God, accept Jesus Christ as your Savior, and walk with him beginning at an early age and throughout your life. That you will love God and pursue Him and follow Him with all your heart, mind, soul and strength and that you will love others as you love yourself. That you will know God's voice and will obey Him and listen to His instruction, and the voice of a stranger, you will not hear nor obey. That you will listen to and be led by the Holy Spirit.

That you will not stray to the right or to the left, but you will walk in the path that He has called you to walk. That you will have favor with God and with man. That you will not lack, but that your needs will be supplied, and you will have more than enough to meet every need. That God will increase you more and more, you and your children.

That you will know your purpose and you will fulfill it. That you will fully develop the gifts and talents that you have been given. That you will trust in the Lord with all your heart and lean not to your own understanding, in all your ways, you will acknowledge Him, and He will direct your path. That you will fear the Lord and depart from evil, and it will be health to your navel and marrow to your bones.

That you will walk in God's protection and that He will deliver you from evil, from sickness and disease, from infirmities, from deception, from hurt, harm and danger. That you will walk in divine health, remain sober, be free from addictions, and have a sound mind. That no weapon formed against you or your family will ever prosper. That God will restore health unto you.

That God will order your steps and give you the wisdom, knowledge, and understanding you need in life. That you will not be bullied nor intimidated. That you will not be fearful. That you will not be insecure or feel inferior to anyone and that you will know who you are in Christ.

That God will give you the right friends and He will let you know who they are, and that you will value and respect them. That at the right time, God will send you your spouse who is born again, who will love you, respect you, honor you, and work along beside you. Your spouse will be someone who will be faithful to God and faithful to you, will build you up and not tear you down, one who will work (be gainfully and steadily employed), and who will love, nurture, raise and be a good role model for your children. Someone who is not a cheater and does not believe or practice multiple marriages. Someone who is not violent – physically, mentally, emotionally, or spiritually -- towards you or your children. Someone whose life honors God.

That you will be a faithful spouse and a role model for your family. That you will not cheat and won't practice multiple marriages. That God will keep counterfeit people and things away from you and will give you the ability to recognize them and stay away from them. That you will love, honor, respect and encourage your spouse.

That you will walk in God's blessings and that no curse will be able to attach itself to you or have any impact on you or your family.

That you will be a mighty woman or man of God that won't be high-minded but will know and acknowledge that without God, you can do nothing, but with Him, all things are possible.

That you will forgive others as God has forgiven you.

That when this life is over, you will hear our Heavenly Father say, "well done, thou good and faithful servant."

The Priestly Blessing for Israel

Numbers 6:22-27 (NIV)

"The Lord said to Moses, Tell Aaron and his sons, "This is how you are to bless the Israelites. Say to them:

The LORD bless you and keep you: The LORD make his face to shine upon you, and be gracious to you: The LORD lift up his countenance upon you, and give you peace. So they will put my name on the Israelites, and I will bless them."

Ideas On How I Can Bless My Family

_____

_____

_____

_____

_____

_____

_____

_____

_____

_____

_____

_____

_____

_____

_____

_____

_____

www.ingramcontent.com/pod-product-compliance
Lightning Source LLC
Chambersburg PA
CBHW070812050426
42452CB00011B/2008